FRUIT OF THE

Spirit

DISCERNING GOD'S EXPECTATION
IN THE LOCAL CHURCH

DR. RICHARD LEE SMITH

Order this book online at www.trafford.com
or email orders@trafford.com

Most Trafford titles are also available at major online book retailers.

Unless otherwise indicated Scripture quotations are taken from the Holy Bible, *New
International Version*®. *NIV*®. Copyright © 1973, 1978, 1984 by International Bible
Society. Used by permission of Zondervan. All rights reserved. [Biblica]

Scripture quotations marked TLB are taken from *The Living Bible* copyright © 1971. Used by
permission of Tyndale House Publishers, Inc., Carol Stream, Illinois 60188. All rights reserved.

Scripture quotations marked KJV are from the Holy Bible, King James Version
(Authorized Version). First published in 1611. Quoted from the KJV Classic
Reference Bible, Copyright © 1983 by The Zondervan Corporation.

Scripture quotations marked NKJV are taken from the New King James Version.
Copyright © 1982 by Thomas Nelson, Inc. Used by permission. All rights reserved.

Print information available on the last page.

ISBN: 978-1-4907-6882-3 (sc)
ISBN: 978-1-4907-6884-7 (hc)
ISBN: 978-1-4907-6883-0 (e)

Library of Congress Control Number: 2016900321

Trafford rev. 09/16/2016

 www.trafford.com

North America & international
toll-free: 1 888 232 4444 (USA & Canada)
fax: 812 355 4082

PURPOSE

To provide resource materials for pastors and parishioners in sermon and Bible study preparations. My intention is to give a thorough theologically-based discussion and understanding of the fruit of the Spirit, as defined in Galatians 5:22–23. I will weave together Scripture, lively illustrations from personal experiences, selected quotes, and stories collected over many years. My hope for the reader is to better discern God's expectation of manifesting the fruit of the Spirit in your life and in your local church.

The fruit of the Spirit is *"love, joy, peace, patience, kindness, goodness, faithfulness, gentleness and self-control."*
—*Galatians 5:22–23 TLB*

DEDICATION

This book is dedicated to my wife, Elaine, who went to be with the Lord on May 9, 2010 after her courageous eleven-year battle with breast cancer. Thank you, Elaine, for your loving support throughout the writing of this book. We all loved you so much. You will remain in our hearts forever.

Jesus said, "Come to me, all you who are weary and burdened, and I will give you rest. Take my yoke upon you and learn from me, for I am gentle and humble in heart, and you will find rest for your souls. For my yoke is easy and my burden is light."
—Matthew 11:28–30

TABLE OF CONTENTS

INTRODUCTION

After forty years, a man stopped going to church. When asked why, he said, "I have heard hundreds of sermons over the years and don't remember any of them, so why go to church?" My response is after over sixty years of eating three meals a day, I can't remember what I ate yesterday, let alone what I ate last week! During my life, I've been nourished by countless meals and am healthy for it. If I had stopped eating years ago, I'm sure I would have died long before now!

This book emerged over many years of sermon preparations, Bible study, and personal prayer life. It developed over an increasing concern to offer a balance between the spiritual gifts and spiritual fruit in the Christian life. I believe a vital ministering congregation should flow from a body of disciples that is growing and producing spiritual fruit. Scripture reminds us, "Thus, by their fruit you will recognize them" (Matthew 7:20).

Billy Graham once commented, "The fruit of the Spirit is God's expectation in our lives. Unlike the gifts of the Spirit, the fruit of the Spirit is not divided among believers. Instead, all Christians should be marked by all the fruit of the Spirit."[1] My intentions here are to study the fruit of the Spirit, examine each one biblically, and attempt to make practical applications to everyday Christian living.

A Christian's life, "as evidenced in Character, should be symmetrical. And while one Christian may show more love for instance than another, or more joy, or a higher standard of faithfulness; still, the nine characteristics of the Spirit's fruit must be developed in some measure in every heart, as the outcome of the life of Christ within."[2]

If there is love, then joy should be seen in one's life. If there is self-control, then gentleness should be apparent. If there is peace, then faithfulness must be evident.

The Spirit that vitalized Jesus' life should also be ours. In Christ, every good quality is blended together. Love should walk hand in hand with joy, peace, patience, kindness, goodness, faithfulness, gentleness, and self-control. Galatians is not the only place where we find a list of "fruit." While there is no official checklist, these fruit do spell out the content of Christian character.

I remember hearing a story in a sermon about a crazy preacher and a wise farmer. It was about a country farmer who was plowing his fields when he heard a car speeding up a dirt road next to his property. He watched as the car spun off the road on a sharp curve. Quite concerned, the farmer ran to the driver and asked if he was okay. The man answered, "I'm okay. I'm a preacher, and I have the Lord riding with me." The farmer said, "Well, you'd better let him ride with me because you're going to *kill* him!"

I love that old hymn, "Tell Me the Stories of Jesus." We can picture those wonderful stories and illustrations from everyday life that Jesus used in His sermons and teachings. Jesus' parables always had relevance to His listeners. He used analogies from ordinary life to bring about spiritual understanding. His teachings were very different from most ancient teachers and philosophers. They used abstract concepts to make things clear.

Plato often spoke about justice; Aristotle used reason, and the Pharisees and Sadducees advocated the law. Jesus simply began with everyday people, turning ordinary lives into something extraordinary. Jesus is Emmanuel or God with us and shows us how to be re-creations in His image.

How do we begin to work this fruit of the Holy Spirit into our daily lives? We must first study and understand through a Spirit-controlled life. We must allow the seeds of these fruit to be cultivated into our daily living. Yes, it will take hard work. It will take constant care and effort. It will take continuous watering of the soul, mind, and body through persistent prayer and delving into God's Holy Word. We should strive to be more Christ-like in all areas of our lives. Remember: the results have eternal rewards.

Placing trust in God's hands applies to people of every age. I will never forget the story told to me by a parishioner before church one Sunday. A little girl saw her pastor baptize a little baby during a Sunday worship service. While playing later that day, she decided to conduct her own baptismal service. She held her cat over a barrel of water and repeated the phrase she had heard in church: "I baptize you in the name of the Father, the Son, and in the *hole you go!*"

As you read this book, it is my hope that, through lively illustrations and theological discussion, you will want to see the fruit of the Spirit – love, joy, peace, patience, kindness, goodness, faithfulness, gentleness and self-control – work in your life. Remember that God produces the fruit; we don't.

Jesus makes an explicit analogy. We can imagine Him standing by a grapevine with His disciples; turning to them, He makes His point perfectly clear. He tells them (and us), "Remain in me, and I also remain in you. No branch can bear fruit by itself; it must remain in the vine. Neither can you bear fruit unless you remain in me" (John 15:4).

Making the analogy even clearer, Jesus says specifically to the disciples, "I am the vine; you are the branches. If you remain in Me and I in you, you will bear much fruit; apart from Me you can do nothing" (John 15:5).

CHAPTER 1

LOVE

A widower lost his only son. One day, he saw his neighbor's house on fire. A young orphaned boy was trapped inside the inferno. The man climbed up an old iron pipe attached to the side of the house and rescued the boy. His hands were badly burned from the pipe. With no living relatives, the people in town wondered who would care for the boy. Only two volunteers came before the town council. One father who'd lost his only son wanted to adopt the orphan. The man who rescued the boy from the fire said nothing. He simply held up his scarred hands. When the council vote was taken, the boy was given to him.

Arnold Prater wrote, "Show me love like God's love, and I will know who lives in you and who produced it."[3] It seems once we are old enough to enter Sunday school, we are taught the simple but powerful words, "Jesus loves me! This I know, for the Bible tells me so." Certainly this most basic teaching of the Christian faith is the sure and certain knowledge of God's love for each of us. But how does the Bible describe God's love?

The New Testament word for love is *agape*. This isn't a word, however, that classical Greek writers commonly used. In Greek, we find there are four words for love. According to William Barclay,

Eros means the love of a man for a maid; it is the love which has passion in it. It is never used in the New Testament at all. Philia is the warm love which we feel for our nearest and our dearest; it is a thing of the heart. Storge rather means affection and is specially used of the love of parents and children. Agape, the Christian word means unconquerable benevolence. It means that no matter what a man may do to us by way of insult or injury or humiliation we will never seek anything else but his highest good. It is therefore a feeling of the mind as much as of the heart; it concerns the will as much as the emotions. It describes the deliberate effort – which we can make only with the help of God – never to seek anything but the best even for those who seek the worst for us.[4]

Love is giving oneself to others, regardless of who they might be or whatever their situation or status in life is. As Christ loved us, so should we love one another.

A young mother found a bill on the breakfast table from her seven-year-old son, Billy. The note read: "Mom, you owe me for running errands, 25 cents; for being good, 10 cents; for taking music lessons, 15 cents; for extras, 5 cents. Total: 55 cents." His mother was amused but said nothing. At lunch, Billy found the bill under his plate with 55 cents and a piece of paper folded neatly. He opened it and read the following: "Bradley owes Mother: for nursing him through the measles, nothing; for being good to him, nothing; for clothes, shoes, and toys, nothing; for his game room, nothing; for all his meals, nothing. Total: nothing."

The apostle Paul puts love first because it's the seed from which all fruit of the Spirit flows. Without love there is no true joy, no peace, no patience, no kindness, no goodness, no faithfulness, no gentleness, and no self-control. Our faith is linked by two commandments: "'Love the Lord your God with all your heart and with all your soul and with all your strength and with all your mind'; and, 'Love your neighbor as yourself'" (Luke 10:27). Love is the fulfillment of God's law.

Billy Graham wrote, "The fruit of the Spirit is love. I cannot love on my own; I cannot have joy, peace, patience, gentleness, goodness, faith, meekness, and temperance by myself. There is no one who has the ability to really love … until he really comes to Christ. Until the Holy Spirit has control of one's life, he doesn't have the power to love."[5]

Love comes first among the fruit of the Spirit because it is divine; God is love, and when we have love, we are most like God. Love is the foundation upon which Christianity is built. Saint Paul says, "And now these three remain: faith, hope, and love. But the greatest of these is love" (1 Corinthians 13:13).

Without love, nothing we do is worth anything. Harry J. Wilmot-Buxton asks, "Can I describe it to you? I might as well try to count the drops in the ocean, or the stars which shine above it, God only knows the love of God. We talk of it, we read of it, we think of it, but we cannot realize it, or understand it."[6]

After many years in the ministry, a pastor went to his file cabinet to pull out the *Love* folder. He soon discovered he didn't have one. Impossible! Surely it must be misfiled somewhere. He searched through *Faith* and *Fasting* and those between *Peace* and *Prayer.* Maybe it was filed between *Caring* and *Christian Education.* Certainly all these have to do with *love,* right? But it wasn't there.

When he paused to reflect for a moment, the Holy Spirit solved the mystery. The *Love* folder was scattered throughout his files; it wasn't misfiled. Parts of it were found under *Hope, Patience, Kindness, Trust, Serving, Healing,* and *Perseverance.* The pastor found the greatest part of his *Love* file centered in *Forgiveness.*

Scripture reminds us that God's love is found in forgiveness. Jesus said, "I tell you that in the same way there will be more rejoicing in heaven over one sinner who repents than over ninety-nine righteous persons who do not need to repent" (Luke 15:7).

As a young boy I remember stealing some tools from a local hardware store to give to my dad for Christmas. It's a wonder I didn't get caught with all those wrenches clanging around in my boots! Years later I felt the need to go back to that store and make restitution. I had planned to repay the cost of the tools plus interest. The only problem was the store had gone out of business. In the midst of all the guilt and shame, I sensed God's abundant love and forgiveness for what I had done. There was no further need to carry that heavy burden from the past. It's a loving God who tenderly searches for sinners and joyfully forgives when they have strayed away.

Mount Everest is the highest mountain in the world. It is 29,000 feet high, reaching five and one half miles into the sky. The greatest ocean depth measured is about 31,000 feet. However, the height and depth of Christ's love for us has never been measured and never will. His love surpasses all knowledge! The apostle Paul writes, "For I am convinced that neither death nor life, neither angels nor demons, neither the present nor the future, nor any powers, neither height nor depth, nor anything else in all creation, will be able to separate us from the love of God that is in Christ Jesus our Lord" (Romans 8:38–39).

God's love is not only beyond measure, but it is eternal. No matter what hardship or fear we may face in life, nothing can separate us from Christ's constant love and presence within us. God's love reaches out and draws people in. The Gospel in miniature reminds us, "For God so loved the world that He gave His one and only Son, that whoever believes in Him shall not perish but have eternal life" (John 3:16).

This sacrificial love brings the entire gospel message into focus in just one verse. It's an unconditional giving of ourselves to others because God first loved us. Have you ever noticed how we can give without loving but can't love without giving? Love is unselfish. Love was never meant to stay in a bottle somewhere, kept only for ourselves, but love was meant to be given away.

I remember one of the seminary professors telling us about a hiker who was thirsty but couldn't find any water until he came to an abandoned house. He found an old water pump and began pumping it with all his might. But there was no water. Then he saw a small jug with a cork in it and a pencil attached. It simply said, "The water in this jug must be poured into the pump to prime it." At first he questioned the note, but when he followed the directions, he had all the cool water he needed to satisfy his thirst. Before leaving, he filled the jug with water so the next thirsty person could have water too. He added to the note, "Believe me, it really works! You have to give it all away before you can get anything back."

Interesting, isn't it, when we help others, we in turn help ourselves? Psalms speaks about God's inexhaustible love. It says, "Give thanks to the Lord, for He is good. His love endures forever" (Psalm 136:1).

We should never have to worry about running out of God's love because the well can never run dry. We often hear the saying, "Love may not make the world go around, but it sure makes the trip worthwhile." Or as someone wrote, "A bell isn't a bell until you ring it. A song isn't a song until you sing it. Love wasn't meant to stay in your heart. Love isn't love until you give it all away." This kind of love is essential in any church family.

What does the Bible have to say about human love? *The New Bible Dictionary* states that love in the Old Testament, "whether human or divine, is the deepest possible expression of the personality and of the closeness of personal relations."[7]

A friend told me the story about a little boy who was frightened by lightning and thunder. He yelled out one night, "Daddy, come in my bedroom. I'm scared!" His father said, "Son, God loves you, and He'll take care of you." The little boy said, "I know God loves me, but right now I want somebody who has skin on." Human love needs to be clothed with those personal relationships of family and friends.

As a child, every Saturday we ate fresh homemade bread and baked beans. My mother always cooked two huge pots full of hot golden-brown pea beans. She also made twenty-one loaves of bread each week to feed our family of seven. It wasn't unusual for us to devour two or three loaves in one meal. I used to love watching the butter melt on my bread. I looked forward to that meal every week. Desserts often included fresh homemade apple pies, mouthwatering cakes with thick chocolate frosting, warm tapioca pudding, and of course *whoopee pies.* Everything always tasted so good!

Before we ate, however, we always joined hands and sang grace together. The grace I remember singing most frequently went like this: "For health and strength and daily food we praise thy name O Lord! Amen!" This song reminds me of the little boy who was asked to say grace at supper one night. He objected by saying, "Why do I have to say grace again? We've already blessed this meal three times!"

I can't imagine life without leftovers. I still think a plate full of hot homemade beans tastes better the next day. I'll always cherish those moments of deep abiding love when we gathered as a family. I will especially remember that big hug and kiss from my parents before going to bed each night. No matter what went wrong during the day, I always knew I had a dad and mom who loved me very much.

The apostle Paul defines real love by saying, "Love is patient; love is kind. It does not envy, it does not boast, it is not proud. It is not rude, it is not self-seeking, it is not easily angered; it keeps no record of wrongs. Love does not delight in evil but rejoices with the truth. It always protects, always trusts, always hopes, always perseveres" (1 Corinthians 13:4–7).

Paul also reminds us that, while people may have different gifts, everyone has the ability to love. Some children were asked, "What is love?" One little girl answered, "Love is when your parents read you bedtime stories, but true love is when they don't skip any pages."

Several Greek words could be translated from the English word *love.* Numerous books have been written on the subject of spiritual love. Many describe different words used for love in Scripture: *agape* – divine love, *phileo* – friendship love, and *eros* – sensual love.

While different kinds of love are described in Scripture, however, love is not to be neatly categorized in Christian life. All love originates in our love for God and His love for us. In *The Way of Christian Living,* John H. Timmerman writes, "Divine love is like the pebble thrown into a still pool. Without that first splash of the pebble striking water there is no action at all; but after the first splash the concentric rings spread out over the water until the entire surface ripples with action."[8]

Philadelphia is called the city of brotherly love. This is a good definition of *phileo*. Phileo, however, is not the word we find in 1 Corinthians 13. The difference between brotherly love and *eros* is "not a distinction in energy but in direction, in object, and in purpose."[9] The word *eros* refers to the love between a husband and wife.

Jay Kesler said of love and sexuality, "Sex, after all, is God's idea. Therefore sexual relationships are important. God has given our sexuality to us for two purposes – to propagate the human race and to teach us about intimacy with other human beings."[10]

A husband and wife were celebrating their fiftieth wedding anniversary. Having spent most of the day with relatives and friends at a big party given in their honor, they returned home. Before going to bed, they decided to have a little snack of tea, bread, and butter. The husband opened up a new loaf of bread and handed the end piece (the heel) to his wife. She was furious! She said, "For fifty years you have been dumping the heel of the bread on me. I won't take it any longer!" On and on she vented her anger over the heel of the bread. Her husband was absolutely astounded. When she finished ranting and raving, he said to her quietly, "But dear, it's my favorite piece."

Over the years, many people learn that marriage is the ability of two incompatible people learning to live compatibly. Sometimes love doesn't always mean staring at each other but having the ability to look outward in the same direction. Paul's letter to the Corinthians reminds us that "Love never fails" (1 Corinthians 13:8).

On the human level, as on the divine, Billy Graham says, "I respect you. I care for you. I am responsible for you. I see you as you are, a unique individual – as we are all unique. I accept you as you are and will permit you to develop as God purposes for you. I will not exploit you for my own benefit. I will try to know you as well as I can, because I know that increased communication and knowledge will enhance my respect for you."[11]

I've heard it said that those who deserve love the least need it the most. The most common Greek word in the New Testament for all forms of love is *agape*. This is one of the "least frequent words in classical Greek, where it expresses, on the few occasions it occurs, that highest and noblest form of love which sees something infinitely precious in its object."[12] Unconditional love comes with no strings attached. It's a gift. The only thing we have to do is receive that love.

A number of years ago, in an institution outside Boston, a young girl known as "Little Annie" was kept locked in the dungeon. The doctors insisted that a dungeon was the only place to put those who were deemed to be hopelessly insane. She lived in a small cage with little light and no hope. However, a nurse nearing retirement believed there was hope for all of God's children. She started taking her lunch into the dungeon and eating outside Little Annie's cage. The nurse believed she might be able to communicate her love and hope to the little girl.

In many ways, Little Annie acted like an animal, often attacking anyone who came into her cage. At other times, she ignored them. Little Annie didn't acknowledge the nurse at all until, one day, the nurse brought some brownies and left them outside her cage. When the nurse returned the following day, the brownies were gone. She brought more brownies when she visited each week.

It wasn't long before her doctor noticed a change in Little Annie. After a while, she was moved upstairs. Finally, the day came when this "hopeless case" was told she could go home. But she didn't want to leave. She wanted to stay and help others in need. You see, it was she who cared for, taught, and looked after Helen Keller. Little Annie's name was Anne Sullivan.

The New Testament writers chose a little-used Greek word for love – *agape* – to express what God wanted to reveal about Himself in Jesus Christ. This is how He wanted Christians to relate to each other. The Bible says, "This is how we know what love is: Jesus Christ laid down His life for us. And we ought to lay down our lives" (1 John 3:16).

Love or, "Agape love, produced by the Holy Spirit, is like yeast; it transforms the one loved. As the Spirit of Christ has transformed Christians, so too, love to others by Christians is not self-sufficiency. It is a fruit of the Holy Spirit, who does it all, with us, and in us. A good analogy is agriculture in which farmers are not passive, but plant, cultivate, fertilize, herbicide, irrigate, and harvest. But – they wait for the growth and maturity to take place."[13]

The Bible reminds us that love is a command. The apostle John wrote, "Dear friend, I am not writing you a new command but an old one, which you have had since the beginning. This old command is the message you have heard. Yet I am writing you a new command; its truth is seen in Him and you, because the darkness is passing and the true light is already shining" (1 John 2:7–8). When Jesus wanted to conquer this world, He simply looked upon it in love.

The Old Testament (Leviticus 19:18) and the New Testament (John 13:34–35) command us to love one another. Our Christian lives should reflect this love by showing respect toward others through self-sacrifice and service (John 15:13). Love should be the glue that holds the Christian church together. Love is often the key that unlocks even the hardest of hearts.

We are to love one another as Jesus loved us. Jesus loved us enough to give His life for us. We may not have to die for someone else, but there are other ways to practice sacrificial love – whether through listening, helping, encouraging, or giving. I'm sure we can think of someone who needs this kind of love today. When we do, we should give all the love we can and then try to give a little more.

Did you know in order to minister to other people we must first learn to give of ourselves? I have often asked myself why so many people today seem to have the attitude reflected in this little poem, which was conveniently placed in the narthex of a church I visited once. It read, "I had a little tea party this afternoon at three. 'Twas very small with three guests in all - just I, myself, and me. Myself ate all the sandwiches, while I drank up the tea, 'Twas also I who ate the pie, and passed the cake to me."

People are so wrapped up in themselves that they can't share their lives with others. Even today, "Love's healing touch is desperately needed in the home, the business, the school, the church, and the government. Therefore, we need to let God fill our hearts with His love. Then we need to share that love with others. Love is life's most precious gift."[14]

Does a plastic heart have love in it? This was a question posed by a young girl to a heart surgeon. He replied with these words: "Yes, a plastic heart has a lot of love in it. It comes from hundreds of people.

They work many long hours so others may live. So think of the hearts involved, and you'll see how much love there is in a plastic heart."

Jesus says, "But I tell you, love your enemies and pray for those who persecute you" (Matthew 5:44). A little girl wrote to her pastor one day. "I remember you said to love our enemies. But I am only six and don't have any enemies yet. So I hope to have some when I am eight. Love from your friend, Amy."

Scripture says our love should choose the path of forgiveness rather than the path of revenge. Oftentimes, however, when someone has wronged us, it seems our first instinct is to get even in some way.

Jesus tells us that we should be good to those who have offended us. We should not keep score, but only love and forgive, as Jesus taught. Perhaps then we need to ask for God's help as we pray for those who have hurt us rather than plan our next attack.

Harry J. Wilmot-Buxton echoes this sentiment by saying, "It may be that some of you who hear me now have quarreled with your neighbors; you never speak now to those who were once your friends; you only talk of them in an unkindly way. You think you do right to be angry; you have been badly treated, badly spoken of. Ah, my brethren, where is your Christianity?"[15]

Does this necessarily mean that, if we dislike someone, we're not Christians? I don't believe so. I'm sure there will always be those we'll disagree with or dislike. We can make a choice to be genuinely concerned for other people while not always feeling affection for them. When we choose to love others, we should trust God to administer that love through us.

I once heard the biggest surprise a man can give his wife on their anniversary is to remember it. At a golden wedding anniversary party for an elderly couple, the husband was feeling moved and wanted to tell his wife just how he felt about her. She was very hard of hearing, however, and often misunderstood what he said. With many family members and friends gathered around, he toasted her. "My dear wife, after fifty years, I've found you tried and true!" Everyone smiled in approval, but his wife said, "Eh?" He repeated the same statement, only louder." His wife shot back, "Well, let me tell *you* something, *mister.* After *fifty* years, I'm *tired* of you too!"

While there's humor in that story, we should never grow tired of loving God. As Christians, we must ask the question of how to love

God. Mark quotes Jesus' words, "The most important one," answered Jesus, "is this: 'Hear, O Israel: The Lord our God, the Lord is one. Love the Lord your God with all your heart and with all your soul and with all your mind and with all your strength.' The second is this: 'Love your neighbor as yourself.' There is no commandment greater than these." (Mark 12:29–31).

To love God is one of the greatest acts we can perform. The whole Bible can be summed up in the rule to love God and love others. We also find these commands in the Old Testament (Deuteronomy 6:5 and Leviticus 19:18). We should include these two commands in every decision we make. They should guide our thoughts and actions in life. In all situations, we should first ask ourselves if a choice best demonstrates our love for God and others.

John W. Sanderson once wrote, "God's enemies enjoy sunshine and rain. If we want to be His children we must live as He does, and do good to all. The next time we meet a particularly repulsive individual and all our self-righteousness wells up within us and we are ready to 'vent our spleen,' we should look up at the sun and the clouds and remember our Father's love. If we hear this word, we will begin to love."[16]

John writes in his gospel, "As the Father has loved me, so have I loved you. Now remain in my love. If you keep my commands, you will remain in my love, just as I have kept my Father's commands and remain in His love. I have told you this so that my joy may be in you and that your joy may be complete. My command is this: Love each other as I have loved you" (John 15:9–12).

Sometimes this love is taken for granted, as in the following story. Ole and Olga lived on a farm in the Midwest. Olga was starved for affection. Ole never gave her any signs of love, and Olga's need to be appreciated went unfulfilled. Frustrated, Olga yelled out, "Ole, why don't you ever tell me you love me?" Ole stoically said, "Olga, when I married you, I told you that I loved you. If I ever change my mind, I'll let you know."

Well, we know that's simply not enough. We need to express our love for one another each day, just as God does for us through His Son, Jesus. Love should be new every day. Remember, three times Jesus asked Simon Peter, "Do you love me?" Peter said, "Lord you know all things: you know that I love you." Jesus said, "Feed my sheep" (John 21:17).

I once heard about a Parisian painter, Marcel de Leclure, who wrote to the love of his life, Magdalene de Villalore. The letter contained the phrase, *"Je vous aime,"* or "I love you" 1,875,000 times. However, he didn't write a single word with his own hand but hired a scribe instead. He could have been lazy and just told the scribe to write it 1,875,000 times. But Leclure loved the sound of those three words so much that he decided to dictate them word for word and had the scribe repeat them verbatim. Altogether, the phrase was spoken and written 5,625,000 times before the work was completed. That's truly a love expressed through time and effort.

When Jesus asked Peter three times if he loved Him, we must also remember that Peter denied who Jesus was three times. Peter was asked three times if he loved Jesus, and each time Peter responded with the word *yes*. It is one thing to love Jesus, but one must be willing to serve Him as well. This is why Jesus told Peter to feed His sheep.

Many lonely sailors have been encouraged by a flashing signal from Minot's light off Scituate, Massachusetts. The signal spells "I love you" in nautical code. A number of years ago, the Coast Guard decided to replace the old equipment. They said, for technical reasons, the new equipment would not be able to flash the "I love you" message. The public protested, and the Coast Guard authorities changed their minds. I understand the old equipment still remains today and continues to send its message of love to all.

Like the flashing signal that spelled those words, "I love you," Peter's love of God would mean a message of service for all to see. Peter's life was forever changed from that moment on. His occupation would change from fisherman to evangelist. He would become known to everyone as Peter, the "rock." This is what a loving God means. He requires a love encompassing everything we have and are. He means we should love Him with all our hearts, souls, minds and strength.

Love is needed in the church. However, it's often the greatest lack in the church. As Christians, we should fill our lives every day with love for others, as God loves us. To love God is to be guided by love in everything we do.

A story is told about a reporter who was at the scene of a burning house. He noticed a little boy standing by with his parents. The reporter said, "Son, it looks like you no longer have a home." The little boy said, "We have a home; we just don't have a house to put it in."

When gathered around the altar, sharing God's Word through a common meal, the church finds humility and love as a wonderful pattern for community. Love is so often what we do. Each year, we celebrated with a "love feast" during worship on the Sunday prior to Thanksgiving. After a brief time in the sanctuary, we walked downstairs to our fellowship hall to continue our worship service. Once seated around tables set with pumpkins, gourds, and other images of fall, we passed food around for all to share.

The love feast or the *agape* meal originally began in the early life of the New Testament church. This first meal was probably eaten in a group setting after Pentecost. The meal is noted in Acts 2:44–47 and in Jude 1:12. The love feast appears to follow the ancient Jewish tradition of the Passover meal. Throughout the years, Christians of all faiths have joined together in this love feast celebration. The meaning of the service is carried out in the words of the hymns.

Early Methodists in England were sometimes left out of the established church. So they began the love feast as a way of celebrating the breaking of bread. Christians often broke bread and drank wine to symbolize and remember Jesus' command to love one another. How true are the words of Catherine Marshall in her book, *The Helper*: "Perhaps the greatest distance any of us ever has to travel is that long trek between the head and the heart."[17]

To the end, God's Word closes with a simple reminder to love one another. The question remains, how do we respond to this outpouring of the Holy Spirit's love in our hearts? How will we show our love for God today? Timmerman concludes "The fruit of *love* grows from the 'True Vine', the central stalk of Jesus in our lives. If the vine withers there, all our spiritual fruit is jeopardized."[18]

CHAPTER 2

JOY

John Newton wrote, "Joy is a fruit that will not grow in nature's barren soil."[19] A story is told of a man who came to a renowned doctor in France. He asked the physician what he could do to get well. The doctor thought of a well-known man named Grimaldi, whose humor was known throughout Paris. The doctor told the man to introduce himself to Grimaldi so that he might enjoy life again. The depressed young man looked up with a scornful smile and said, "I *am* Grimaldi."

How can joy become a characteristic in our lives? Joy should grow out of genuine worship of God. Through worship we not only have celebration but confession. I believe God encourages us to take ownership of this joy in our lives. God's intention for religion is to celebrate and not only for meditation and contemplation. While reflection and confession are important, we should not forget to celebrate everything God has done and is still doing for His people.

The Greek word for joy is *chara*. Joy is the "presence of God manifested in a consistent gladness of heart, and from awareness that serving others has met or may meet needs."[20]

A happy couple always raised cucumbers and made sweet pickles together. The husband just loved to watch his garden grow. He even spent his winters studying the seed catalogues to get the best possible cucumbers. The whole family enjoyed preparing the soil, planting seeds, and caring for the plants.

His wife loved to make sweet pickles. She often studied the best recipes and the best methods of preparing and preserving them. They were such a happy family, and many visitors went home with a jar of their famous pickles. The church always had a good supply of their pickles on hand. People loved the fact that this family found a project to do together.

Finally, the man died. The next spring, all the children returned home. They said to their mother, "We know how much you love making pickles, so we are going to prepare the garden and plant them for you." The mother smiled and said, "Thanks a lot, children, but you don't have to do any planting because I really don't enjoy making pickles. I only did it because your father loved to grow the cucumbers."

The children were stunned. The youngest son was really upset, however, since the father had pulled him aside not too long before he died and told him he really didn't like growing cucumbers; he only did it to please his wife!

Well, is this a happy or sad story? I'm not sure. In many ways, I suppose, it's a happy one. While they were happy *doing* for each other, people also enjoyed being with them. Why is it also a sad story? Primarily because they were not able to share their changing needs and joys with each other. Instead of growing, they stagnated in doing what they thought were their duties to each other.

William Barclay wrote, "It is not the joy that comes from earthly things, still less from triumphing over someone else in competition. It is a joy whose foundation is God."[21] Our spiritual joy should not only be a privilege, but it should also be a duty.

The words *joy* and *rejoice* are most often used to translate the Hebrew and Greek words into English. In fact, joy is found over 150 times in the Bible, while words such as *joyous* and *joyful,* if included, number over two hundred. The verb *rejoice* appears well over two hundred times as well. The Bible says, "Rejoice in that day and leap for joy, because great is your reward in heaven. For that is how their ancestors treated the prophets" (Luke 6:23).

A seminary professor once told our class about a preacher who was addressing his congregation one Sunday. He was trying to impress upon them the importance of religion. He yelled from the pulpit, "All you people of this congregation," "one day, you're going to die! Do you hear me? All you people are going to die!" One little man sitting in the front pew started to laugh, so the preacher asked him, "What's so funny?" The man answered, "I don't belong to this congregation!"

Often, "true joy is full of sweet and holy calm; it anchors the soul in peace and safety amidst all the changes and chances of this mortal life, and all the storms of earth."[22] The question should be asked: how can this kind of joy become a description of our lives? The Psalmist writes, "I keep my eyes always on the Lord. With Him at my right hand, I will not be shaken. Therefore my heart is glad and my tongue rejoices" (Psalm 16:8–9).

The Bible encourages God's people to be filled with joy. We should continually increase our levels of joy. This joy comes to us by being in the presence of God. David was happy because he learned the secret of this joy. A lasting, true joy is one that comes from God's living presence within us.

At this point, we should distinguish between the words *happiness* and *joy*. Happiness is only a temporary condition, whereas joy, as stated above, is based on God's presence within His people.

After a worship service one Sunday, an old lady stopped and spoke to the pastor who had only been with the congregation a few months. She said, "I'm deaf, and I can't hear a word you say, but I still come to get my plate full." Hoping to console her, the pastor said, "Well, maybe you haven't missed much." She replied, "Yes, that's what they all tell me."

Oftentimes, I use humor to illustrate a point in my sermons. Sometimes I wonder if my congregation misses the point, especially when no one laughs at the punch line. Stephen Bayne once wrote, "Our Lord seems never to have hesitated to sharpen a picture or underline a teaching with a touch of humor."[23]

Speaking of humor, a woman shared the following story with me after church one Sunday. She told me about her daughter who climbed up on the lap of her great-grandmother. As she looked at her white hair and wrinkles she asked, "Did God make you?" "Yes," she said. Then she asked, "Did God make me too?" Great-grandma said, "Yes." "Well," said the little girl, "Don't you think He's doing a better job now than He used to?"

I've heard it takes seventy-two muscles to frown and only fourteen to smile. Perhaps there is truth in the wise old adage, "Friendship doubles our joy and divides our grief." Did you know that a twelve-year-old girl in Winnipeg, Canada, holds the record for the longest smile in the world? She held a smile for ten hours and five minutes!

Joy comes from having the Holy Spirit in us. Jesus said, "Remain in Me, and I will remain in you. No branch can bear fruit by itself; it must remain in the vine. Neither can you bear fruit unless you remain in Me" (John 15:4).

It should be noted that "the peculiar wonder of Christianity is that Christians have a Savior who wants joy! Jesus is so in touch with our common, human condition – having walked with His people and, beyond question, having laughed with them – that He desires nothing more than that our joy, be made full. It is a rare and wonderful thing among the many religions of the world that Christianity cherishes humor, laughter, and joy."[24]

Apart from Christ, we cannot expect this fruit of the Spirit to grow in us. While imitating Christ before others, we must continually work at joining our lives to Him through our knowledge of and love for Him. I believe the secret of Christian joy is to live in Jesus Christ, just as the branch abides in the vine. Our energy source and sense of security are based in Christ.

Chapter 15 of the gospel of Luke is probably the most famous biblical reference to God's joy. Here the Pharisees and scribes criticize Jesus for receiving sinners and eating with them. Then Jesus tells three parables about the lost sheep, the lost coin, and the lost son. The explicit theme of each parable is the joy felt when even one sinner repents.

On his sixteenth birthday, a son approached his father and asked, "Dad, I'm sixteen now. When can I get my license, so I can drive the family car?" His dad looked at him and said, "Son, driving the car takes maturity; first, you must prove you are responsible enough. One way you can do that is to bring up your grades because they are not acceptable. Second, you must read the Bible every day. And finally, I want you to get a haircut because your hair looks awful!"

So the son began fulfilling his father's requirements, knowing that the last request might be impossible. When his grades came out, he went to his dad with a big smile. "Look, Dad, I have all A's and B's on my report card. Now I can finally drive the car!" "That's excellent, son; you are one-third of the way there, but have you been reading the Bible?" the father asked. "Yes, Dad, every day," his son said. "That's very good; you are two-thirds of the way there. Now, when are you going to get that hair cut?" Thinking he could outsmart his dad, the son responded, "Well, I don't see why I should get my hair cut to drive the car. Jesus had long hair, didn't He?" His father looked at him and said, "That's right, son, and Jesus walked everywhere He went too!"

Joy runs through the entire biblical account of the coming of Christ. The most familiar passage is the angel's announcement in the advent season of "good tidings of great joy, which shall be to all people" (Luke 2:10 KJV). What Christmas season would be complete without singing Isaac Watts' hymn, "Joy to the World"? Remember those words: "Joy to the world, the Lord is come!"? Have you ever noticed that there is an exclamation point at the end of that sentence? This is because our faith unites our hearts to Christ, which, in turn, makes us participants in His joy.

A little boy listened carefully one Sunday as his teacher explained why Christians give presents to each other on Christmas day. She said, "The gift is an expression of our joy over the birth of Jesus and our friendship for each other." When Christmas came, the boy brought the teacher a special seashell. The teacher asked, "Where did you ever find such a beautiful shell?" The boy said there was only one spot in a certain bay several miles away where such beautiful shells could be found. His teacher said, "Why, it's gorgeous! But you shouldn't have gone all that way to get a gift for me." The little boy smiled and said, "The long walk was part of the gift."

Joy is that "lively pleasure of the soul which we feel in the possession of present good, or the certain expectation of good in the future."[25] The real meaning of Christmas is indeed "good news that will cause great joy for all the people" (Luke 2:10). It's Christ who puts the joy into Christmas and all the year through.

Jesus illustrated the kingdom of heaven by telling the story of the joyful man who found treasure (Matthew 13:44). The Bible says Zacchaeus joyfully received Jesus after being called down out of a tree. Each found that life's real treasure is in Jesus Christ.

Many years ago, a little boy was given a priceless possession – his deceased grandfather's gold pocket watch. How he treasured it! One day, however, while playing at his father's ice plant, he lost the watch in all the ice and sawdust. He searched and searched but found no watch. Then he realized what he needed to do. He stopped running around and became very quiet. In the silence, he heard the watch ticking.

God has given each of us a priceless gift of joy in Jesus Christ. How easy it is to lose our joy in the hustle and bustle of life, especially during the Christmas season. Yet it's always there to find if we just pause and listen to that wonderful presence of Christ in our hearts. Jesus never promised us the gift of joy in a neatly-wrapped package. For, "joy needs to be nourished with heavenly manna. The flame must be replenished off God's altar, or it will soon burn dim, and at length expire."[26]

An electric company disconnected the power to a home for non-payment. That day an unusual notice appeared at their door. It read, "We would be delighted if you would pay your bill promptly. If not, you will be de-lighted."

I wonder how many hearts are *de-lighted* of Christ and void of the true meaning and message of the Christmas season instead of being *delighted* in Christ. I believe we should try each day to bring joy into someone's life, even if it means leaving that person alone once in a while. Philippians reminds us to be joyful in spite of the circumstances surrounding us. "Rejoice in the Lord always. I will say it again: Rejoice!" (Philippians 4:4).

Well, how can people experience joy in their lives when circumstances are rough? It seems joy is also linked with challenges we face. Sometimes God tests our faith, even allowing us to be stretched to the limits. However, we can also experience renewed rejoicing through a deep, abiding faith.

The disciples found this type of faith when they were physically attacked or verbally abused for following Jesus. An inner joy often filled them as a result. The knowledge that God's purposes were being fulfilled in their lives made them joyful. The Bible says, "The apostles left the Sanhedrin, rejoicing because they had been counted worthy of suffering disgrace for the Name" (Acts 5:41).

I find it amazing how the apostle Paul could tell the church to rejoice from his prison cell. Paul's joy was complete, no matter what circumstance he found himself in because he knew Jesus was always with him. On a number of occasions, Paul urged the Philippians to be joyful. For many, just the thought of going to prison would lead to discouragement.

Dr. Viktor Frankl, author of *Man's Search for Meaning*, was imprisoned by the Nazis in World War II because he was a Jew. His wife, children, and parents were all killed in the holocaust. The Gestapo made him strip naked at the concentration camp. While cutting off his wedding band, Viktor said to himself, "You can take away my wife, you can take away my children, you can strip me of my clothes and my freedom, but there is one thing no person can ever take away from me – and that is my freedom to choose how I will react to what happens to me!"[27] Isn't it interesting that, even under the most difficult of circumstances, joy can still be a choice in transforming our tragedies into triumphs?

Most of us have experienced what happens to motorists when one of those huge graders goes to work on a highway repair job. When the machine is operating on a busy road, traffic is stopped, and vehicles line up in opposite directions. A veteran operator of one of those big machines decided one day to relieve the tension that inevitably results from traffic backup. On both ends of his grader he attached signs reading, "The road to happiness is almost always under construction."

We often want to base our lives on circumstances around us rather than trusting in God. I wonder how many people pursue happiness as a goal in life. I wonder how many become disappointed along the way. Often, "happiness is shy and elusive, and those who seek it directly, rarely find it. Real happiness, deep and abiding, that is, joy, is a by-product of love. Go after it and it evades and escapes you. Live for others and it comes to you unsought and unawares."[28]

The Psalmist reminds us to "Worship the Lord with gladness; come before Him with joyful songs" (Psalm 100:2). I once heard a pastor say in a sermon, "When you talk about heaven, let your face light up with a heavenly glory. When you talk about hell, your everyday face will do." That's why it's so important to know we have a choice about the joy we feel. Unfortunately, there are many who feel they have no choice.

How many times have you gone into a store and said to a clerk, "Hello" or "Good morning"? The clerk offers to help but doesn't really appear to be enjoying his or her work. When you ask how the clerk enjoys the job, the clerk responds with, "I hate it!" It appears the clerk only works there out of necessity – just putting in the time. When we serve God, how many of us just put our time in without having a real sense of joy in our hearts? Are we merely serving our Lord out of a sense of duty rather than abundant joy?

A third grade teacher was getting to know her students on their first day of school. She began by asking a question to see how her students felt. The question was, "What makes you happy?" Every teacher, I am sure, wants happy students. After all, who wants to live eight hours a day with sad faces? One third grader answered, "I want a computer. A computer would make me happy." Another child responded, "Barbie and Ken dolls make me happy." A third student said, "Recess makes *me* happy!"

As we reach out to others in Jesus' name, we should remember that the Holy Spirit's supply of joy is inexhaustible. Jesus says it's "A good measure, pressed down, shaken together and running over, will be poured into your lap. For with the measure you use, it will be measured to you" (Luke 6:38). The key to experiencing joy with others so often begins not with the question of what do I need but with what can I do?

The Bible says, "The joy of the Lord is your strength" (Nehemiah 8:10). A nine-year-old with leukemia was given six months to live. As the doctor told her parents the diagnosis outside the hospital room, she overheard his words. However, she didn't fully understand her condition. To everyone's surprise, her faith in Christ gave her an attitude of victory. She talked freely and with hopeful anticipation about her death. As she grew weaker, her joy became more radiant. One day, before going into a final coma, she said to her family, "I am going to be the first to see Jesus! What would you like me to tell Him for you?"

What does it mean personally for us to know we have a God who laughs? Perhaps the greatest source of Christian joy lies in the fact that this world is not our final home. This life is not the end. The New Testament closes with a picture of the most wonderful joy a Christian can have: "a new heaven and a new earth" (Revelation 21:13–17).

Jesus didn't call us to the *good life,* as measured by today's standards. He didn't promise us a certain quality of life. He didn't even promise we would always be happy. He did, however, call us to a life of servanthood and gave us His promise of joy.

Christian joy comes only from our eternal and loving God. What a joy to one day stand before Jesus, hearing His words, "Well done, good and faithful servant! You have been faithful with a few things; I will put you in charge of many things. Come and share your master's happiness!" (Matthew 25:23). It's said that "the real reward given to the faithful believer is *joy.* Salvation begins with *joy* and ends in *joy.*"[29]

CHAPTER 3

PEACE

While painting *The Last Supper,* Leonardo da Vinci became very angry with a man watching him. He even threatened him. When he went back to paint the face of Jesus, he couldn't continue because of all the bitterness welling up inside. A lack of peace in his heart forced him to put down his brushes, go find the man, and ask for his forgiveness. Only then was Leonardo able to have enough inner calm to finish the face of Christ.

What is peace? Peace or *eirene* in Greek is defined as "a quietness and confidence from God by being right with Him (righteousness), an antidote to fear, resentment, distress, guilt, and inter-personal differences."[30]

The Old Testament describes peace as spiritual completeness, security, soundness, or well-being. It's used when we ask about or pray for the welfare of another person. The Bible says, "Pray for the peace of Jerusalem: May those who love you be secure. May there be peace within your walls and security within your citadels" (Psalm 122:6–7).

This kind of peace is more than the absence of conflict. It suggests wholeness with God and one another. It's a peace of health, justice, protection, and prosperity the world can't provide. Real peace comes only through faith in God. When we find peace with God, we find peace of mind and peace with others. Peace, however, doesn't always mean we escape from the stresses in this life.

Jesus says, "Peace I leave with you; my peace I give you. I do not give to you as the world gives. Do not let your heart be troubled and do not be afraid" (John 14:27). A deep and lasting peace is a result of the work of the Holy Spirit in our lives. Unlike worldly peace, this kind of peace assures us confidence in all circumstances. With Christ's peace in our hearts, we have nothing to fear from the past, present, or future. Peace is resting in God's power, not our own.

When Jesus was born, the angel said to the frightened shepherds, "Glory to God in the highest heaven, and on earth peace to those on whom His favor rests" (Luke 2:14). We know the world has seen very few years of peace since Christ, our Prince of Peace, came.

> A sparrow once asked a dove, "Tell me the weight of a snowflake." "Nothing more than nothing", was the answer. "In that case, I must tell you a wonderful story", the sparrow said. "I sat on the branch of a fir, close to its trunk, when it began to snow – not heavily, not in a raging blizzard – no, just like in a dream, without a sound, and without any violence. Since I did not have anything better to do, I counted the snowflakes settling on the twigs and needles of my branch. Their number was exactly 3,741,952. When the 3,741,953rd dropped onto the branch, nothing more than nothing, as you say, the branch broke off." Having said that, the sparrow flew away. The dove, since Noah's time, an authority on the matter, thought about the story for awhile, and finally said to herself, 'Perhaps only one person's voice is lacking for peace to come to the world.'[31]

The Bible has much to say about peace. This is evident in the fact that the term occurs four hundred times. The Bible is often seen as God's testament of peace. We can have the peace of God (Philippians 4:7), peace with God (Romans 5:1), and peace from God (2 Corinthians 1:3). God the Father is the God of peace who will sanctify the believer (1 Thessalonians 5:23). God the Son is the Prince of Peace, on whose shoulders the spiritual government will rest (Isaiah 9:6). God the Holy Spirit produces the fruit of peace in the life of the believer (Galatians 5:22).

Scripture assures us that when our ways please the Lord, God makes our enemies at peace with us (Proverbs 16:7). At Jesus' birth, angels praised God by saying, "Glory to God in the highest heaven, and on earth peace to those on whom His favor rests" (Luke 2:14).

Of all the Bible verses about peace, however, my favorite is in Isaiah. It reads, "You will keep in perfect peace those whose minds are steadfast, because they trust in you" (Isaiah 26:3). This verse provides personal inspiration, as well as strength.

Peace often calms internal conflict. We should first, however, acknowledge the anxiety that lives within us. We should ask ourselves about the source of our worries and frustrations. Only after such self-examination are we able to fully invite our loving God to produce His peace in us. We cannot fully understand the meaning of peace until we know how it affects our souls. Our ability to cope with inner conflict is so often determined by the level of peace we receive from God.

Imprisoned in Caesarea, Paul writes to the Philippians. "Do not be anxious about anything, but in every situation, by prayer and petition, with thanksgiving, present your requests to God. And the peace of God, which transcends all understanding, will guard your hearts and your minds in Christ Jesus" (Philippians 4:6–7). Paul is referring to the weed of anxiety. "Anxiety is the preoccupation with things of lesser importance, in the false confidence that if they are well cared for, life will move smoothly along."[32]

A simple formula to enjoy peace with God is found in Philippians 4:6–7. In brief, it says we should be anxious for nothing, prayerful in everything, and thankful for anything. Remember that peace doesn't always guarantee us freedom from anxiety. As Christians, we're not taught that life is to be without struggle, pain, and suffering.

Peace is a calming influence for internal conflict. Sin, fear, failure, doubt, and many other forces wage war within us. God's peace moves our hearts and lives by holding those hostile forces at bay, while offering comfort in times of conflict. Jesus says He will give us this peace if we accept it from Him. We receive this peace through the Comforter or Holy Spirit. It often comes in our times of greatest trials and tribulations – when the storms of life rage all around us. We must first have God's peace within us before we are able to offer it to anyone else.

One of the saddest places on earth is a cemetery of unclaimed dead found in New York City's Potter's Field on Hart Island. It received several hundred poor, homeless, and stillborn bodies each year. They were delivered by truck and ferry from all over the New York City area. The number of burials since 1869 is nearly one million. Often the pallbearers were prisoners from the city's workhouse on the 101-acre island. The bodies arrived at the cemetery in pine coffins, each with its own number. The only marker at Potter's Field is a single monument with the word *Peace*. It's somewhat misleading, however, since few of those buried there ever found peace on this earth. Whatever reward they may have will be in heaven.

Cemeteries are often seen as places of loneliness, sadness, and despair. The Bible, however, says that the cemetery will one day be the liveliest place on earth. When Jesus returns to earth, the graves will open, and the dead will be raised. This of course is that great message of Paul to the Corinthians.

> Listen, I tell you a mystery: We will not all sleep, but we will all be changed in a flash, in the twinkling of an eye, at the last trumpet. For the trumpet will sound; the dead will be raised imperishable, and we will be changed. For the perishable must clothe itself with the imperishable; and the mortal with immortality. When the perishable has been clothed with the imperishable, and the mortal with immortality, then the saying that is written will come true: "Death has been swallowed up in victory." "Where, O death is your victory? Where, O death is your sting?"
>
> —1 Corinthians 15:51–55

Where volcanoes exist, people from around the world say that the area around them for miles is often barren and burnt up by volcanic fire. No grass, bushes, or trees grow in these black desert regions, but here and there, in the cracks, flowers seem to bloom out of nowhere. This is true on the Big Island in Hawaii. Through all the volcanic ash and ruin, life begins anew.

High in the Andes mountains stands a bronze statue of Christ. It's made from old cannons, and its base is granite. It marks the boundary between Chile and Argentina. Engraved on it in Spanish are the words, "Sooner shall these mountains crumble into dust than Argentines and Chileans break the peace sworn at the feet of Christ the Redeemer."[33] This monument is a reminder that only Jesus can bring true peace to the world.

Remember: Jesus rode on a donkey rather than a horse on Palm Sunday for a good reason. In ancient times, the horse was considered a symbol of war, whereas a donkey was the symbol of peace. Scripture says, "Therefore, since we have been justified through faith, we have peace with God through our Lord Jesus Christ" (Romans 5:1).

Peace is reconciliation with God. We can all have peace with God; it's sometimes different from peaceful feelings such as calmness and peace of mind. Peace with God is possible because Jesus paid the price for our sins through His death on the cross. George Washington once said, "To be prepared for war is one of the most effectual means of preserving peace."[34]

While riding the bus to school one day, our youngest daughter told us about a boy who was being picked on by some older students. In fact, they had been throwing spitballs at him. This taunting seemed to amuse everyone except our daughter, a high school junior at the time. Immediately, she left her seat and sat next to the boy being teased. It wasn't long, however, before both were being pelted with spitballs.

Deciding she had had enough of their fun and games, she quickly turned around and yelled, "You guys had *better* knock it off! The next one that hits either one of us again will have to deal with *me!* I've studied *karate,* you know!" Since no one wanted to test her, they immediately stopped teasing them. The funny thing about this story is our daughter had only taken one karate lesson in her whole life!

It's said that those with clenched fists cannot shake hands. I have studied the martial arts off and on for almost thirty years. I have a black belt in the Kempo style of karate. The word *karate* quite literally means "empty hand." Some people look upon this sport as being aggressive or violent. However, karate has enabled me to have greater physical health, as well as the ability to defend myself if needed. It was certainly a change from regular parish duties. Of course, I don't advocate violence, nor would I recommend such resolve toward conflict resolution.

The following illustration came to me from an old church newsletter clipping a number of years ago. It's about a man who was sitting in a café when, all of a sudden, someone came in and beat him up. When he woke up, he said to the owner, "Who was that?" The owner said, "That was Kung Fu from China." The next week, the man was eating in the same café when a different man came in and beat him up. When he woke up, he said to the owner, "Who was that?" The owner said, "That was Kuan Chow from Taiwan." Several weeks later, Kung Fu and Kuang Chow were eating in the café. The man who had been beaten by both of them came in and beat both of them up. He said to the owner, "When they wake up, tell them that was a hammer from Sears!'"

My karate instructor once said, "The open hand holds more friends than the closed fist." The motto of the Apollo 11 flight was "We come in peace for all mankind." This motto was imprinted on the plaque left on the moon. The landing was on the Sea of Tranquility. Armstrong and Aldrin found a peaceful place to land. The name is appropriate, since there has never been anyone there to disturb the peace.

No wonder Jesus often went alone into the hills to pray. Peace can certainly be found, even if momentarily, in places offering us a change from everyday routines and the demands of life. Peace is a rare commodity at times. It can pass all understanding, according to the Bible. Albert Einstein once said, "Peace cannot be kept by force. It can only be achieved by understanding."[35]

Speaking of a peace that passes all understanding, November twenty-seventh each year marks the anniversary of Alfred Bernard Nobel's will. Why is the date of a will so important? His will left the bulk of a huge fortune from his invention of dynamite and other explosives to award achievers in various disciplines: the Nobel Peace Prize.

"In 1867, at age 34, Nobel was granted a patent for dynamite and over the next 29 years of his life he became fabulously wealthy from the manufacture of explosives. His will, dated November 27, 1885, provided for a trust to establish 5 prizes in the field of peace, physics, chemistry, physiology or medicine, and literature. Recipients of the prizes were to receive a gold medal, a citation diploma, and cash awards from $30,000 to $40,000. A sixth award in economic science was added in 1969."[36]

I find it interesting that "since 1919, the nations of Europe have signed more than 200 treaties of peace. Each treaty, simply another scrap of paper, was broken more easily than consummated. From the year 1500 B.C. to A.D. 1860 more than 8,000 treaties of peace, meant to remain in force forever, were concluded. The average time they remained in force was two years."[37]

Many times in church I have sung that wonderful hymn, "Let There Be Peace on Earth." Remember the words: "Let there be peace on earth, and let it begin with me; let there be peace on earth, the peace that was meant to be." The Bible reminds Christians that the rewards are great for those who strive for peace. In the Sermon on the Mount, Jesus said, "Blessed are the peacemakers: for they shall be called the children of God" (Matthew 5:9 KJV). One might ask how this peace is achieved. How can we find this peace?

An elder parishioner told me the following story. It's about a young man named Anderson and an old man named Patterson. Both had grocery stores on the same block. Eggs were the subject of their frequent price wars, with Anderson at one time lowering the price of eggs by one-half. The next day, Patterson reduced his price by the same amount. On the third day, Anderson lowered his price by another third. This exchange continued until Anderson finally went to the older man in frustration and said, "I surrender. We've both been selling eggs at a loss for a long time." "Not me", laughed Patterson. "You see, I've been buying my eggs from *you!*"

The Bible says, "Who would have said to Abraham that Sarah would nurse children? Yet I have born him a son in his old age" (Genesis 21:7). Peace is so often a by-product of our trust in God. After repeated promises, a visit by two angels and the appearance of the Lord Himself, Sarah finally cried out with joy at the birth of her son. The way to bring peace to a person's troubled heart is to focus on God's promises.

True peace is found when we are most active in doing God's work. As a gift of God, Christians should be willing to actively seek out God. Scripture says, "Now is the time to do it, while the Lord is blessing us with peace… Let us build and fortify cities now, with walls, towers, gates, and bars. So they went ahead with these projects very successfully" (2 Chronicles 14: 7 TLB).

We should note that peace is a by-product of obedience. Asa's reign was marked by peace because he was careful to obey God. This theme of obedience is often repeated in Chronicles. Obedience to God leads us to peace with God and others. With Judah's kings, obedience to God led to national peace, just as God had promised centuries earlier.

In our case, obedience may not always bring peace with our enemies. It will, however, bring complete peace with God in our eternal home. One of the first steps on the path to peace is to obey God. We must learn to trust God through every stressful moment of life. The Bible says, "Because of the Lord's great love we are not consumed, for His compassions never fail. They are new every morning; great is your faithfulness!" (Lamentations 3:22–23).

Jesus often speaks about comfort and peace. He says, "Come to me, all you who are weary and burdened, and I will give you rest" (Matthew 11:28). Sometimes "God's people mostly have to go through the hottest fire of affliction, and to suffer most, just as the most precious stone has to bear the sharpest cutting and the hardest polishing."[38]

The word *peace* occurs often in the New Testament. In fact, according to my research, it's found in every book except 1 John. Its biblical roots, however, are clearly found in the Old Testament. The word *shalom* has deep meaning and is God's special promise to us. Shalom is "a peace that exists in spite of circumstances. Shalom is a peace that exists because we find our wholeness and our security in our relationship with God."[39]

Even the Psalmist found peace while walking in "the valley of the shadow of death." (Psalm 23:4 KJV). We too can find peace around us just where he found it. "I will fear no evil: for thou art with me" (Psalm 23:4 KJV).

Many times, we ask ourselves how in the world there can ever be peace. It's a world where planes bomb and slaughter innocent people. Children are molested, and police are ambushed. Gangs control the streets while drug lords corrupt whole neighborhoods. It's a world of bombings and beheadings, a time of fear and fighting.

Years ago, it was other wars. Next year, it will be another group somewhere else. It's a time when employers and employees have to watch their backs. We see husbands and wives unwilling to compromise to bring about healing through conflict resolution. We hear, "Just leave me alone, and don't get in the way of what I want."

John W. Sanderson points out that "The first element in the peace which God gives, then, is the peace of friendship, of a breach removed, of a relationship restored. And when we remember that the relationship restored is between the eternal God and one of His creatures, and that this restoration was effected by God Himself in full conformity to the law, then this peace is seen to be complete, eternal, and sweet beyond comprehension."[40]

A visitor to Israel said,

> You cannot understand shalom until you hear it spoken amid
> all the signs of war in Jerusalem. Only then does the deep sense
> of promise and of hope come through. This is probably true of
> most of the significant words in the Bible; we must be careful
> to understand them, as far as this is possible, in their ancient
> usage. We may well ask, has the modern Israeli captured the
> full biblical significance of the term? In the Scriptures 'shalom'
> sometimes means little more than 'hello,' 'good-by,' 'never
> mind.' It can, more significantly, denote order, absence of
> strife, good health. Sometimes it is equivalent to 'salvation,'
> 'reconciliation to God.' And 'heaven.'[41]

The Psalmist writes, "I cried out to the Lord, and He heard me
from His Temple in Jerusalem. Then I lay down and slept in peace and
woke up safely, for the Lord was watching over me" (Psalm 3:4–5 TLB).

Peace is also a by-product of our dependence on God. How often
we find that sleep does not come easily during times of stress and
conflict. Surely King David must have had some sleepless nights when
his son, Absalom, rebelled and gathered an army to kill him. Scripture,
however, tells us that David slept peacefully, even during the rebellion.

What made the difference? When David cried out to the Lord, the
Lord heard him. The assurance of answered prayer can often bring
peace. It's easier to sleep at night, knowing that our loving God is in
control of all areas of our lives. You see, if we stay awake and worry
all night about things we can't change, it's then we should be thanking
God for being in control. When we do this, we can sleep well.

It's good to have peace of mind. Peace is one of God's best gifts to
us. It seems, in many ways, the other spiritual gifts depend on it. Today,
more than ever, there is a global hunger for peace.

The book, *Peace with God*, by Billy Graham, has sold millions
of copies in many languages; it's an indication perhaps of how much
peace is needed in our world. In some languages, such as Arabic
and Hebrew, the standard greeting is "peace," as mentioned earlier.
However, until we fully have Christ in our hearts, we can never know
this true peace.

Someone shared this advice with me several years ago: "What we eat doesn't give us ulcers; it's what's eating us." It is true. Perhaps what we really need is a peace conference with the Prince of Peace.

William J. Armitage asks, "What is true peace? It is not necessarily freedom from outward cares. God does not promise His people entire immunity from care. But He does teach us the way to rise above it, and to possess peace in the midst of the anxieties of life. The surface of Lake Superior is often swept by storms, but the tempest's rage affects only its surface. In its great depth – 900 feet deep – calm reigns. The same contrast is seen in a Christian life ruled by trust. It has its outward trials, but is has also its inward peace."[42]

The Bible states, "So when all these things begin to happen, stand straight and look up! For your salvation is near" (Luke 21:28 TLB). A complete and true peace will only come when Jesus Christ returns. The picture of the coming persecutions and natural disasters seems very gloomy, but we don't have to worry.

When, as Christians, we see these events happening, we will know that the return of our Messiah is near, and we can look forward to Christ's reign bringing justice and peace. While we should be concerned about what's happening in our world today, we should also be waiting with confidence for Christ's return to bring justice and restoration to His people everywhere.

The biblical Jesus was a man who was often surrounded by controversy. He said, "I did not come to bring peace, but a sword" (Matthew 10:34). Harry J. Wilmot-Buxton observed that "the world can give a man pleasure and self-indulgence. It whispers – 'Eat, drink, and be merry.' It bids a man drown care in strong drink; forget troubles in excitement and dissipation. And he does forget for a time, but he does not find peace."[43]

Sometimes we find ourselves making costly mistakes, as in the following story. A teenager worked as a delivery boy for a florist. One day, he had two floral arrangements to deliver; one was going to a church for the dedication of a new building and the other was going to a funeral home. He got confused and took the arrangements to the wrong locations.

The florist received a call from an angry minister. "We've got a basket of flowers in the front of our new sanctuary that says "Rest in Peace." The florist replied, "You think you've got problems! Somewhere in this town there is a casket with flowers beside it that says "Good luck in your new location!" Some mistakes are more serious than others, but disregarding the gospel message is the biggest mistake of all!

Speaking of new locations, a retired couple was worried about the threat of nuclear war, so they studied all the inhabited places around the world. They wanted to know where they could find the least likely place to be affected by war, a place of security and peace. They studied and traveled all over the globe until they finally found the right location. So on Christmas day, they sent their family and friends cards from their new home in the Falkland Islands. As we know, Great Britain and Argentina soon turned their paradise into a war zone.

Jesus reminds us again, "Peace I leave with you; my peace I give to you. I do not give to you as the world gives. Do not let your hearts be troubled and do not be afraid" (John 14:27). We should never forget that Jesus, as the Prince of Peace, came preaching peace. He died on the cross to make peace possible for all His people. Jesus' life is the conduit through which God's love is given, as heralded the night He was born.

Scripture teaches us that peace is a common attribute of God's kingdom. In all circumstances, "Let the peace of Christ rule in your hearts" (Colossians 3:15). We should ask Jesus to give us peace as expressed in this prayer: "Now may the Lord of peace Himself give you peace at all times and in every way. The Lord be with all of you" (2 Thessalonians 3:16).

As mentioned before, the Hebrew word for peace was both an appropriate and common greeting for those living during New Testament times. Jesus often used phrases such as "Go in peace" and "Peace be unto you." It was more than a greeting, however, because Jesus' use of the term implied His delivery and conditions of peace. When Jesus sent the twelve disciples to the surrounding towns and villages, He told them, "As you enter the home, give it your greeting. If the home is deserving, let your peace rest on it; if it is not, let your peace return to you" (Matthew 10:12).

In early Bible times, eating together after a disagreement meant a token of reconciliation, which often healed broken relationships. Jesus left us His peace in the sacrament of Holy Communion. This was His last earthly and dying gift of love to us.

If peace is a fruit of the Spirit, that fruit also needs to be nurtured. Identify one area of your life in which you must particularly pray for and nurture the fruit of peace. Is there a relationship with an individual that needs healing, where peace must be restored? Pray specifically for that relationship. To be peace bringers to others, Christians must first of all be at peace with themselves and with God. Sometimes hurting memories must also be healed. This too can be brought to prayer. Since Jesus is the pattern for our Christian walk, we do well to think of specific actions of Jesus that restored peace.[44]

God's love bridges the gap of separation between Him and His people. Jesus paid the penalty for our sins when He died on the cross and rose from the grave. The Bible says, "He personally carried the load of our sins in His own body when He died on the cross" (1 Peter 2:24 TLB). Therefore, we should respond by receiving Jesus Christ into our hearts by faith. It's then that we close the gap and cross the bridge into God's family.

The gospel of John says, "Yet to all who received Him, to those who believed in His name, He gave the right to become children of God" (John 1:12). To receive peace in Christ, we need to do four things: admit we are sinners, repent and turn away from our sins, believe that Jesus died for us on the cross, and then receive Christ into our hearts through prayer.

Finally, we should consider Robert Fulghum's advice in his book, *All I Really Need to Know I Learned in Kindergarten.* "Think what a better world it would be if we had cookies and milk about three o'clock every afternoon and then lay down with our blankies for a nap. Or, if all governments had as a basic policy to always put things back where they found them and to clean up their own mess. And it is still true, no matter how old you are – when you go out into the world, it is best to hold hands and stick together."[45] So let us go now in *peace*, with the love of God surrounding us.

CHAPTER 4

PATIENCE

A train was filled with tired people. Most spent the day traveling through hot, dusty plains. When evening came, everyone tried to settle down for a good night's sleep. However, one man was holding a tiny baby who was restless and began crying loudly. Unable to sleep, a big man spoke up for the rest of the group. "Why don't you take that kid to its mother?" There was a pause for a moment, and then the father replied, "I'm sorry. I'm doing my best. The baby's mother is in her casket in the baggage car ahead." There was a deafening silence for a moment. Then the big man got out of his seat and walked toward the man with the crying baby. He apologized for his unkind remark and impatience. He took the tiny baby in his own arms and told the tired father to get some sleep. All through the night, he cared for the little child with loving patience.

Patience (*makrothumia*) is a "calm endurance or perseverance not easily provoked by suffering or questionable conduct of others."[46] *Makrothumia* was a great word to use for patience. First Maccabees 8:4 says it was by *makrothumia* that the Romans ruled the world. This meant that the Romans, in their persistence, would never make peace with an enemy – even in defeat. That kind of conquering patience was generally used toward people rather than events or things. Its use is commonly seen in God's attitude toward humanity (Romans 2:4, 9:22; 1 Timothy 1:16; 1 Peter 3:20).

William Barclay wrote that God could "have wiped out this world long ago; but He has that patience which bears with all our sinning and will not cast us off. In our dealings with our fellow men we must reproduce this loving, forbearing, forgiving, patient attitude of God toward ourselves."[47]

Following a sermon on patience one Sunday, a visiting pastor shared the following experience with me. He told me about a long line of cars filling up a huge parking lot where he was attending a church conference. As he parked, he noticed the word *love* on a light post in one area. In another section, he saw the word *faithfulness*. The next day, he pulled into a different lot at the same church and saw the word *patience* on another sign.

Just like numbers in a mall parking lot, those words helped people find their cars. No doubt, they served another purpose as well. After each meeting, some people actually cut each other off in the parking lot in their efforts to rush home. Patience obviously wore thin, and tempers flared. How appropriate those signs are for us today. I find it amazing how quickly our love and patience disappear in a parking lot for those we profess as our brothers and sisters in Christ!

Dr. Isaac Barrow called Christianity "the academy of patience. We need to remember that in the school of Christ the Holy Spirit is the great Teacher."[48] A seminary professor told our class how Martin Luther would read the Bible while praying that his heart would be filled with love for all people. How quickly that love disappears when a person with offensive body odor sits down beside us!

Saint Francis de Sales once said, "Be patient with everyone, but above all with yourself."[49] It's interesting that the testing of our faith doesn't always come through cruel oppression or heavy burdens. It's more likely to occur in the checkout line, on the turnpike, or in a parking lot. That's where we know whether or not we've really become serious about our faith in Christ.

What does the Bible tell us about patience? The Bible tells us in the book of Genesis that God's patience has limits. The Lord said, "My Spirit will not contend with humans forever, for they are mortal; their days will be a hundred and twenty years" (Genesis 6:3). God was allowing the people of Noah's day 120 years to change their sinful ways.

God also shows His unending patience with us. He gives us time to stop living selfishly and begin living His way through His Word. While 120 years may not seem long, time eventually began to run out, and the earth was flooded. Our time is running out too. Consequently, we need to turn to God for the forgiveness of our sins. While we cannot see God's timeline on patience, we know there is little bargaining power for additional time.

Speaking of additional time, a friend told me the following story. (It has a way of stopping us right in our tracks.) As the story goes, an old train was slowly creeping through a valley when it suddenly stopped. The only passenger was a salesman riding the train for the first time. He asked the conductor why he had stopped so suddenly. The conductor said, "It's nothing to worry about, sir. There's a moose on the tracks." Several minutes later, the train got under way again, but after chugging along for a few miles, it stopped abruptly once more. The conductor said, "Just a temporary delay. We'll be on our way very soon." The annoyed salesman asked, "What's going on now? Did we catch up to that moose again?" Sometimes we too are impatient with God's schedule.

Why do tires go flat or engines overheat when we are in a hurry to get to an appointment? Why does our furnace stop running in the middle of a cold winter night? More importantly, why do we get so unhappy and frustrated when things like this happen? We're not only impatient with God's timetable but ours as well. Richard F. Houts said, "Yet, though on God's timetable, He wants us to 'be patient in well-doing,' not passive. The farmer doesn't simply wait for a crop, without doing his work."[50]

The fruit of patience is found in the character of God. We should note that Peter, an impatient man himself, describes God's patience in at least three places in the Epistles (1 Peter 2:20, 3:20, and 2 Peter 3:9). We learn in these passages that patience must be cultivated, as in Jesus' parable of the unmerciful servant in Matthew 18:21–35. In verse 21, Peter wanted to put a limit on human patience when he said, "Lord, how many times shall I forgive my brother or sister who sins against me? Up to seven times?" (Matthew 18:21). In answering, Jesus tells the story about a steward whose master responded without limit to the man's request for patience.

Interestingly enough, that same steward showed no patience to a fellow servant asking him for patience in repaying his debt. Jesus adds, "In anger his master turned him over to the jailers to be tortured, until he should pay back all he owed. This is how my heavenly Father will treat each of you unless you forgive your brother or sister from your heart" (Matthew 18:34–35). This passage teaches us God's patience is powerful and without limit.

There's a story about a truck driver who dropped in at an all-night restaurant in the western US. The waitress had just served his meal when three drunken bikers came in and asked him for a fight. One grabbed his hamburger, and another took a handful of his french fries, while the third picked up his coffee and drank it. The trucker didn't respond as one might predict. Instead, he calmly got up from the table with his check, left his money at the cash register, and walked outside. As the waitress took his money, she watched the man drive away in a big truck. When she returned, one of the bikers said, "He's not very tough is he?" She said, "I don't know much about that, but I know he's not much of a truck driver because he just ran over three motorcycles in the parking lot."

The Bible uses two different Greek words for patience. One has to do with things or endurance, as mentioned in Romans 5:3–4. The other has to do with people and is sometimes translated as "longsuffering." The apostle Paul uses this word in Galatians 5:22. Therefore, "long-suffering, as a Christian grace, looks beyond the instrument to the Hand that guides it."[51]

The book of Nehemiah shows God's patience is found in longsuffering. It says, "They refused to listen and failed to remember the miracles you performed among them. They became stiff-necked and in their rebellion appointed a leader in order to return to their slavery. But you are a forgiving God, gracious and compassionate, slow to anger and abounding in love. Therefore you did not desert them" (Nehemiah 9:17).

It's amazing to see how God continues to be with us – His people – in spite of our repeated failures, pride, and stubbornness. God is always ready to forgive us; His Holy Spirit is always ready to teach us. God's forgiveness helps us forgive those who mistreat us, even if it means "seventy-seven times," as Jesus reminds us.

Somewhere in England many years ago, a young soldier was tried in a military court and sentenced to death. He was to be shot at the ringing of the daily curfew bell. His fiancée climbed the bell tower several hours earlier and tied herself to the bell's huge clapper. When the curfew came, only muffled sounds came from the bell tower. The officer in charge ordered the bell to stop ringing. When his soldiers went to investigate, they found the young woman, cut and bleeding from being thrown around by the bell. The officer was so impressed with her willingness to suffer for her fiancé that he released the soldier and said there would be no ringing of the curfew bell that night.

Patience sometimes means having the assurance of calm and peace during whatever storms arise. Impatience, on the other hand, can rob us of God's joy. It can lead to broken spirits, leaving us irritated and short-tempered. So why do we give in to impatience? What makes us so frustrated and upset when things don't go our way?

As parents, we expect our children to pick up a glass of milk without spilling it. When they don't, we get angry. What we fail to realize is that many young children simply haven't developed the physical coordination skills necessary to do certain functions. We should expect our children to spill things once in a while.

Christians often have unrealistic expectations of God. We ask after praying, "Why hasn't God answered me yet?" "Immediacy is another root of impatience. We are more likely to be impatient with people if we expect to achieve goals immediately rather than through a process."[52]

The writer of Hebrews seems to have this in mind when he says, "You need to persevere so that when you have done the will of God, you will receive what He has promised" (Hebrews 10:36). Billy Graham wrote, "Because impatience is a characteristic of the 'old nature', the 'put off – put on' principle should be practiced. Impatience is a response that must be 'unlearned.'"[53] When one eleven-year-old boy was asked what he wanted most from his parents, he simply responded, "I'd like them to be more *patient* with me."

Speaking of impatience, I remember when my oldest daughter began to ride her new bicycle for the first time without training wheels. I was so happy to see the time had finally arrived for her to ride on her own unaided. Every time I gave a little push to get her started, it was not long before she fell to the ground. Over and over we did the same routine. Each time I pushed, she fell. Soon my joyful anticipation turned into impatience.

I remember becoming very upset with her because she couldn't ride her bicycle the way I thought she should. She cried in total frustration. Little did I know, she just wasn't physically ready to ride yet. It wasn't long, however, before she learned to ride her bicycle. As I looked out the kitchen window one morning, I saw a smiling little girl riding her new bicycle down the street all by herself!

It's clear that "patience is part of the fruit of the Holy Spirit, and it must grow in Christian parents, as it must in all Christians. However, its growth is neither automatic nor magical. Patience must be cultivated along with all other qualities that should characterize

Christians. Christian parents develop patience the same way as everybody else – by acknowledging its importance and working on it."[54]

Driver's education certainly had its challenges for me. Oftentimes, I volunteered my wife to practice with our children on back roads and in parking lots. Since then, I have realized this difficulty may be hereditary. My dad actually refused to drive with me after I drove the family car up on the church lawn!

Robert Gage once wrote, "When a person exercises longsuffering, he can conquer problems that normally would defeat him. It is easy to find reasons why other people should be patient but very difficult for us to be patient. There are times when God asks nothing of His children, except silence, patience and tears."[55] In the midst of longsuffering, we should ask ourselves whether or not we are willing to be silent. It's appropriate to see that 'love in action' is also referred to as longsuffering.

The longsuffering of God is found in almost every page of the Bible. We see it in God's dealings with His people. "Christ also suffered for us, leaving us an example that we should follow in His steps. How patiently did He endure all the sorrows of His lot, the fickleness of friends, the rejection of His own, the contradiction of sinners against Himself, the agonies of anticipated suffering, the mockeries of His ignominious trial, and the tortures of His cross! At any moment He might have prayed the Father and legions of angels would have flown to execute vengeance upon His cruel enemies and false friends, yet did He suffer long with all."[56]

We often ask ourselves why God allows suffering to occur in the first place. Why do the innocent suffer? Certainly many questions and doubts are raised here. "Suffering affliction has been the furnace in which God has ever refined the gold of His saints. How patient must the righteous Abel have been with his cruel and malignant brother! How patient must Noah have been during that one hundred and twenty years, when the ark was a building, and his preaching met with nothing but scorn."[57] God can teach us about longsuffering.

When speaking of patience, we often think of Job. He resented what happened in his life. "He passionately questioned the conventional and orthodox arguments of his so-called friends. He passionately agonized over the terrible thought that God might have forgotten or forsaken him. There are few men who have spoken such passionate words as Job. But the great fact about Job is that in spite of his barrage of questions that tore at his heart, he never lost faith in God. He said, 'Though He slay me, yet will I trust Him.'"[58]

It's good that suffering is limited in both measure and time. Many stories in the book of Judges show how the people of Israel suffered because they failed to follow God. He was so loving and patient with Israel, just as He is with us. However, we must not confuse God's patience with approval of our sins. We should be wary of demanding our own way because sometimes it comes with painful consequences. "Patience is not always a virtue – especially when you are in quicksand."[59]

My wife once made a cross-stitch wall hanging saying, "Please be patient with me, God isn't finished with me yet." John Timmerman adds, "This understanding is also essential to understanding patience. Christian patience roots not in our own life and action but in God's grace to us. We can be patient because God has been patient and gracious to us. We can endure the hard roads of life because God has shaped the way. The very key to patience lies in the knowledge that our goal is not rooted in this life but in eternal life."[60]

We find this same assurance in Paul's letter to the Thessalonians. "May the Lord direct your hearts into God's love and Christ's perseverance" (2 Thessalonians 3:5). As one pastor told me, "A minister sees people at their best, a lawyer sees people at their worst, and a doctor sees people as they are."

Our patience should follow Jesus' model of perseverance. While striving for it might seem to be an unattainable goal, we should still practice patience. As the apostle Paul says, "But if we hope for what we do not yet have, we wait for it patiently" (Romans 8:25). Many schools around the world teach these valuable lessons. Only one, however, can teach us to have patience in times of trouble, and that is the school of Jesus Christ.

A reporter was interviewing a widow who had successfully raised a very large family. In addition to having six children of her own, she also adopted twelve children. Through it all, she provided a stable home life with an air of confidence. When asked what her secret was, she gave a surprising answer. She said, "I managed so well because I'm in a partnership!" "What do you mean?" the reporter asked. The woman said, "Many years ago, I said, 'Lord I'll do all the work and I will always trust you,' and I haven't worried since."

If a "gardener lets the trees in the garden, or the plants in the greenhouse, grow wild and luxuriant at their own sweet will, he knows that there will be little or no fruit or blossom next year. So he cuts them back. It seems hard, perhaps, that those wide-spreading limbs and branches should be pruned and cut so close, look next season, and you will find the roses thicker and stronger, the fruit more abundant."[61]

John and Charles Wesley were blessed with a very patient mother. At one time, her husband said, "I marvel at your patience. You have told that child the same thing twenty times!" Susanna Wesley looked fondly at the child. She said, "Had I spoken the matter only nineteen times, I should have lost all my labor."[62]

We see this illustration of God's patience in the story of the prodigal son. The Bible says, "So he returned home to his father. And while he was still a long distance away, his father saw him coming, and was filled with loving pity and ran and embraced him and kissed him" (Luke 15:20 TLB).

In the two previous stories found in Luke's gospel, the seeker actively looked for the coin and the sheep, which couldn't return on their own. In this story, however, the father watched and waited. While dealing with a son who had a will of his own, the father was clearly ready to greet him if and when he returned home.

In the same way, God's love is stable, patient, and always ready to welcome us home again. He searches for us and gives us many opportunities to respond, but He doesn't force us. Like the father in this story, God also waits patiently for us to come home. John William Reeve adds, "Faith takes up the cross, Love carries it cheerfully, and binds it to the heart, and 'Longsuffering' and 'Meekness' carry it patiently to the end."[63]

A preacher once quit the ministry after twenty years and became a funeral director. When asked why he changed occupations, he said, "I spent three years trying to straighten out Ralph, and he's still an alcoholic. Then I spent six months trying to straighten out Betty's marriage, and she filed for divorce. Then I spent two and a half years trying to straighten out Greg's drug problem, and he's still an addict. Now, at the funeral home when I straighten them out, they stay straight!"

Maurice L. Draper said,

The natural reaction to injury is retaliation. The classic description of this human urge is expressed in the Mosaic Law provision of 'an eye for an eye and a tooth for a tooth.' It is frequently quoted as scriptural justification for retaliation. The spirit of retaliation is contrasted by the Lord with redemptive patience. (Jesus said), 'But I say to you, do not resist one who is evil. But if anyone strikes you on the right cheek, turn to him the other also.' Too often this principle is interpreted as a manifestation of weakness. But the Lord's intention was surely not that a man should abase himself because of fear. He was himself the great example.[64]

Thomas Oden adds, "The pastor does not need always to control or set the direction of the conversation. With patience, the dialogue will offer its own opportunities."[65]

A story is told about a rich baker who sent for twenty of the poorest children in town. He said to them, "In this basket is a loaf of bread for each of you. Take one and come back every day, and I'll give you more." The children immediately began fighting over who would get the largest loaf. Grabbing the bread quickly from the basket, they left without even saying thank you to the baker. Emily, a poorly-dressed little girl, waited patiently until the others had gone. Then she took the smallest loaf left in the basket, kissed the old man's hand, and went home. The next day, the same scenario was repeated. However, this time, when Emily's mother sliced the loaf, she found many shiny pieces of silver inside. When Emily took the money back to the baker, he said, "No, my child, it isn't a mistake, I put them into the smallest loaf to reward you."

The Bible shows us how we can strengthen our patience through difficulties. Moses says that he "went back to the Lord. 'Lord,' he protested, 'how can you mistreat your own people like this? Why did you ever send me if you were going to do this to them? Ever since I gave Pharaoh your message, he has only been more and more brutal to them, and you have not delivered them at all!'" (Exodus 5:22–23 TLB). As the Pharaoh increased the Hebrews' workload, Moses began protesting against God for not rescuing His people. Moses wanted quick results without all the problems. So often when God is at work, suffering and hardships still occur.

James teaches us to be happy when difficulties come our way. By trusting God, our problems can help us develop patience and character. We can also honor God through any present situation. It reminds us that God will not abandon us in our times of need. We should constantly watch with hopeful anticipation for God's plan to work in and through us.

Through the years, I have saved many one-liners given to me by church members. Here are a few on the topic of patience. Someone once said, "Dear God, please grant me patience. And I want it right now!" A Persian Proverb states, "Have patience! All things are difficult before they become easy." The quotation I like best comes from Bill Gotherd: "Patience is accepting a difficult situation without giving God a deadline to remove it."

This is certainly true in the following story. A man's car stalled in the heavy traffic as the light turned green. All efforts to start the engine failed, and motorists behind him made matters worse by honking. Finally, he got out of his car and walked back to the first driver and said, "I'm sorry, but I can't seem to get my car started. If you'll go up there and give it a try, I'll stay here and honk your horn for you."

"Patience," it's said, "is steadfastness in obedience to God despite pressure to deny Him. Where love and joy and peace are lacking, it is difficult to resist invitations to explode in impatience. The world is full of pressures; they are here because of sin; they are here because of the curse which God has placed on the world and its activities. God's people are not immune to them: 'In the world you will have tribulation.' To His Father, Jesus said, 'I do not pray that you should take them out of the world, but that you should keep them from the evil one.' This is the greater reason then for seeking God's grace which will see us through times of difficulty."[66]

Sometimes we even have difficulty understanding our children. Someone once said, "Babies are really great. They have a digestive apparatus with a loud noise at one end and no responsibility at the other." A father reprimanding his child for doing something wrong finally said in exasperation, "Every time you're bad, I get another gray hair." The little guy looked at his dad and said, "Wow! You must have been a terror! Look at Grandpa!" As parents, we may forget the problems we caused *our* parents.

Harry J. Wilmot-Buxton asks, "How can we best learn the lesson of being patient in tribulation? Do not meet trouble half way, and tire yourselves out before you are called upon to bear it. Some people are always looking out for the storm clouds, even on the finest day, and spoiling their happiest hours by anticipating trouble. Take the sunshine and the shower as they come, and believe that the same loving God sends both. Then keep very close to God."[67]

A young Christian man went to an elder member of the church to ask for prayer. "Will you please pray that I may be more patient?" he asked. The old saint agreed. They knelt together, and the man began to pray, "Lord, send this young man tribulation in the morning; send this young man tribulation in the afternoon, send this young man ..." At that point, the young man yelled out, "No, no, I didn't ask you to pray for tribulation. I wanted you to pray for patience!" The wise Christian man replied, "But, it's through tribulation that we learn patience."

We are reminded always to have patience. Over the years, I've learned some things get difficult before they become easy. Shakespeare asks, "How poor are they that have not patience! What wound did ever heal but by degrees?"[68] We can certainly learn a lesson in the degrees of patience from the honeybee, often described as "busy."

Here are some interesting statistics about bees compiled by James S. Hewett in his book, *Illustrations Unlimited*.

To produce one pound of honey, the bee must visit 56,000 clover heads. Since each head has sixty flower tubes, a total of 3,360,000 visits are necessary to give us that pound of honey for the breakfast table. Meanwhile, that worker bee has flown the equivalent of three times around the world. To produce one tablespoon of honey for our toast, the little bee makes 4,200 trips to flowers. He makes about ten trips a day to the fields, each trip lasting twenty minutes average and four hundred flowers. A worker bee will fly as far as eight miles if he cannot find a nectar flow that is nearer. Therefore, when you feel that persistence is a difficult task, think of the bee.[69]

It's said that "patience is a calm willingness to accept and endure provoking and irritating situations and persons. It is a prolonged restraint of anger or outburst (Colossians 3:8). It is recognizing that God has a timetable for each process in our lives. Like Jesus' parable of the growing seed (Mark 4:26–29)."[70]

Each of us – whether mild mannered or hot tempered – should learn to develop genuine biblical patience. When we get angry about something, we often tend to lose our patience with people. We should remember: there will be many challenges to face and problems to solve in life. God frequently uses them to help us help others.

It's like the man pushing a cart with a screaming baby at the supermarket. As he goes up and down the aisles, he softly says, "Keep calm, George. Don't get all excited George. Don't yell, George." A lady, who was watching with approval said, "You certainly need to be commended for your patience in trying to quiet little George!" The man said, "Lady, I *am* George!"

Harry J. Wilmot-Buxton said,

We must have trodden the rough road of suffering ourselves before we are fit to guide others along it. It is said that the makers of the best violins abroad produce their wonderful music by breaking and skillfully mending new instruments, which when first made had little power or melody. When God breaks us with a hard trouble, He knows how to mend us again, and we give forth the music of gentleness, love, and unselfishness, which we were incapable of before. Have you ever watched men mending a road in our great towns? The heavy steamroller crushes down all the sharpness and roughness of the stones, and makes an easy way for people to travel on. So God sends us trials and afflictions which crush the hard, sharp points of our character, and make us fit to help others on the journey from earth to Heaven.[71]

If patience is a virtue, it seems many people today have lost it. In this up-to-the-minute information age, there are few things people are willing to wait for. As people hurry into the future, waiting becomes less of an option. In contrast, however, God always waits patiently for us. Patience can be developed as we wait to let God step in when it does us the most good.

The race is not always about who is the fastest, as illustrated by the story of the turtle and the hare. Patience is so often a matter of timing as we wait for God's plan to unfold in our lives. The Psalmist reminds us to "Be still before the Lord and wait patiently for Him ..." (Psalm 37:7). Sometimes delay is much better than having a disaster.

Scripture says, "You too, be patient and stand firm, because the Lord's coming is near" (James 5:8). James uses the illustration of a farmer patiently waiting for his land to produce crops. He doesn't simply sit around doing nothing, but he prepares the soil, sows various seeds, and keeps his fields weed-free. As the germination process takes place and the plants grow, the farmer waits patiently, trusting in God's nurturing hand. Patience so often is a matter of watchfulness with hopeful anticipation.

Oftentimes, "patience is the most tragically misunderstood fruit of the Spirit. Perhaps for that very reason, it may also be one of the most profoundly important. Impatience is probably one of the most common human weeds."[72]

Thomas Edison believed that patience is measured not by the hours invested but by what has ultimately been accomplished. I've heard that Edison always kept a clock on his desk without hands. He believed the rewards of work called for 2 percent inspiration and 98 percent perspiration. Even a great genius knew the persistent art of patience.

In his book, *Seeds of Greatness*, Dennis Waitley concurs. "Victory takes persistence. It took twenty-two years for the McDonald's hamburger chain to make its first billion dollars. It took IBM forty-six years and Xerox sixty-three years to make their first billion. If only we would apply that kind of determination to our walk with God!"[73]

I saved a quotation from a preaching seminar in which Zig Ziglar said,

> I'm such an optimist I'd go after Moby Dick in a rowboat and take the tartar sauce with me." It was explorer, Fridtjof Nansen, who was "lost with one companion in the Arctic wastes. By miscalculation they ran out of all their supplies. They ate their dogs, the dog's harnesses - the whale oil for their lamps. Nansen's companion gave up and lay down to die. But Nansen

did not give up. He told himself, "I can take one step more." As he plodded heavily through the bitter cold, step after step, suddenly across an ice hill he stumbled upon an American expedition that had been sent out to find him.[74]

That story of perseverance and waiting patiently reminds me of a time when I was lost for three days in Newfoundland, Canada. I attempted to hike seven miles to an old abandoned fishing village called Deer Harbour. It wasn't long, however, before I noticed a heavy fog rolling in around me. Not only did I find myself traveling around in circles, but I had also run out of food. Without a compass or food or idea of where I was, I prayed like never before.

While praying on the third day, I noticed the sun beginning to poke through the dense cover of fog. As I walked back, I noticed an orange juice can I had left on a tree branch three days earlier. From that point, it took only twenty minutes to reach home. Amid the tears and anger of awaiting family and friends, I learned that the Royal Canadian Mounted Police were organizing a search party for me. I won't do that again!

Ecclesiastes says that patience is worth the wait.

There is a time for everything, and a season for every activity under the heavens: a time to be born and a time to die, a time to plant and a time to uproot, a time to kill and a time to heal, a time to tear down and a time to build, a time to weep and a time to laugh, a time to mourn and a time to dance, a time to scatter stones and a time to gather them, a time to embrace and a time to refrain from embracing, a time to search and a time to give up, a time to keep and a time to throw away, a time to tear and a time to mend, a time to be silent and a time to speak, a time to love and a time to hate, a time for war and a time for peace. He has made everything beautiful in its time.

—Ecclesiastes 3:1–8, 11

Our generation lacks patience. Billy Graham wrote, "This is a high-strung, neurotic, impatient age. We hurry when there is no reason to hurry, just to be hurrying. This fast-paced age has produced more problems and less morality than previous generations, and it has given us jangled nerves. Impatience has produced a crop of broken homes, ulcers, and has set the stage for more world wars."[75] Impatience seems to cover a wide range of issues in our lives. We are impatient with family and friends, impatient when certain goals are not accomplished, and even impatient while waiting for our prayers to be answered.

A man once attended his pastor's farewell service; the pastor had faithfully served his congregation for thirty years. Several clergy members attended, each eloquently celebrating the pastor's qualities and accomplishments. However, the pastor said he had forgotten everything they said except for a simple comment by a man who wasn't even scheduled to speak. With permission, the man stood and said, "I have seen my pastor nearly every day of my life for thirty years, and I've never seen him in a hurry!" After the service, the pastor said it was the best compliment he had ever received. Only then did he truly understand what it meant to "wait patiently upon the Lord."

What are some things that make us feel frustrated and impatient? Could it be waiting in a checkout line, sitting in slow traffic, getting your children to bed, putting up with poor utility service, waiting in a doctor's office, being patient with someone not returning your call, listening to door-to-door salespeople, or trying to get your car started? Is there an area of your life where you tend to lose patience quickly? How can you change that? How can you develop more patience in your life?

The Bible doesn't focus on our feelings or on how frustrated we are. It centers on our ability to bring about those actions and attitudes that move us beyond our current condition into more hopeful and helpful experiences. Our example of patience must come from God. "Because God is in control there is victory in patience. It is always a comfort to feel that others have gone through what we have to go through."[76]

The Bible tells us we can develop patience through hardships. Second Thessalonians 1:4 TLB says, "We are happy to tell other churches about your patience and complete faith in God, in spite of all the crushing troubles and hardships you are going through." Clearly the apostle Paul was persecuted during his first visit to Thessalonica (Acts 17:5–9). There's no doubt that those who responded to his message and became Christians continued to be persecuted.

In Paul's first letter to the Thessalonians, however, he said Christ's return would bring deliverance from persecution and judgment. This statement caused the people to expect Jesus to return soon to rescue them. So Paul taught them to wait patiently for God's kingdom and to learn perseverance and faith through suffering.

Patience is described as the ability to 'keep on keeping on.' In the process of developing the electric lamp, Edison failed over three thousand times before inventing the light bulb. He performed many experiments with countless materials. When each one failed, he would toss it out the window. The pile of failed experiments reached the second story of his house. Then he sent people to China, South America, Asia, Japan, Jamaica, Ceylon, and Burma to search for the right fibers to be tested in his laboratory. After thirteen months of repeated failures, on October 21, 1879, the fatigued Edison succeeded in finding the right filament to sustain electricity.

You see, Edison refused to admit defeat. He continued to experiment for two days and nights without sleep. Finally, he put a carbonized thread into a vacuum-sealed bulb, and he turned on the current. His persistence, after so many disappointments, has given our world electric light!

Billy Graham once said, "Patience is the ability to absorb strain and stress without complaint, to be left undisturbed by obstacles, delays, or failures. God allows difficulties, inconveniences, trials, and even suffering to come our way for a specific purpose. They help develop the right attitude for the growth of patience. As the Christian sees these trials producing beneficial, character-building results, the stage is set for the development of a patient spirit. God the Holy Spirit will then be able to produce the fruit of *patience* in his or her life."[77]

CHAPTER 5

KINDNESS

Following a spanking one night, a father returned to his son's bedroom to encourage and scold him. "I really didn't want to spank you, but the Bible says that children should obey their parents. While crying, the little boy said, "I know, but the Bible also says, 'Be ye *kind* to one another' too, Dad!"

Why does God expect us to be kind to one another? The Bible says, "But love your enemies, do good to them, and lend to them without expecting to get anything back. Then your reward will be great, and you will be children of the Most High, because He is kind to the ungrateful and wicked" (Luke 6:35).

Kindness is often "the way or manner in which we treat others, including expression of biblical words such as listening, compassion, agape love, mercy, forgiveness, etc."[78] When we show kindness toward others, we imitate God's love in our lives. Love means action.

One way we put love to work is by taking the initiative to meet specific needs. This is easy to do with people who love us and with those we trust. However, love also means showing acts of kindness to those who dislike us or want to hurt us. We should give as though we are giving to God.

"Kindness (*chrestotes*) is relating in a supportive, tender, and caring manner to others in need of ministry."[79] The "Greek word translated, 'kindness', in Galatians originally carried the notion of usefulness. In time the expanded concept of moral excellence was added. Thus it became one of the main words in Greek which denotes goodness."[80] I've heard it said that a person cannot do a kindness too soon because one never knows how soon it will be too late!

A woman's gravestone had the following words inscribed: "Buried at age sixty-eight, died at age seventeen." What this really meant was that she had received little kindness from those closest to her (family and friends) since the age of seventeen. She had been constantly put down with words and actions that were demeaning and alienating.

John Wesley wrote, "Do all the good you can, by all the means you can, in all the ways you can, in all the places you can, at all the times you can, to all the people you can, as long as ever you can."[81]

To better understand what kindness is, we should take a look at how it's used in the Bible. The writers of the Old Testament saw God's kindness expressed in nature (Psalm 65:9–15); in history (Psalm 145:107); in God's Word (Psalm 119:65–68); in affliction (Nahum 1:7); for the poor (Psalm 68:10); for those who trust God (Psalm 34:8); and for those who fear Him (Psalm 31:19).

The New Testament also shows examples of God's kindness, even to those who are ungrateful (Luke 6:35; Matthew 5:45). It is seen in the act of God sacrificing His Son so that we would have salvation now (Titus 3:4–7) and in the ages to come (Ephesians 2:7). Because God is kind to us, we should be kind to one another.

In a television interview, Mother Teresa once commented that the biggest disease today isn't leprosy or cancer. It's a feeling of being abandoned, unwanted and alone. It's a lack of love and charity toward others. It's like being left by the side of the road at the end one one's life.

I will never forget when our youth group acted out the parable of the Good Samaritan one Sunday. All the parts were quickly spoken for, including the donkey. But no one volunteered to be beaten and left for dead, as was the traveler on the road. After the Sunday school lesson on the Good Samaritan, a teacher asked her students, "What would you do if you saw a man bleeding beside the road?" One little girl quickly said, "I'd throw up!"

Have you ever asked someone a question and that person answered you with a question? It seems strange, right? However, one of the most beautiful stories in the Bible is there because a lawyer asked Jesus some questions. First he asked, "What must I do to inherit eternal life?" The lawyer answered the question himself by saying, "Love the Lord your God with all your heart and with all your soul and with all your strength and with all your mind, and, 'Love your neighbor as yourself.'" Then he asked, "And who is my neighbor?" (Luke 10:25–29). Jesus answered with the story of the Good Samaritan.

Over the years, some parishioners have shared with me some very funny stories. One woman told me about a Sunday school teacher who was reading the story about the Good Samaritan. She asked the children why the Levite passed by on the other side. One little girl said, "Because the poor man had already been robbed!"

Speaking of robbers, I heard about a bank teller who had just been robbed for the third time by the same man. The investigating officer asked if she had noticed anything in particular about the thief. She said, "Yes, he seems to be better dressed each time!"

Several years ago, I found myself in the middle of a bank robbery in northern New Hampshire. As I attempted to cash a check, I noticed only one other customer in the bank with me. The teller said the computers were down, and I would have to wait in the lobby. While waiting there, a man dressed in a long raincoat started a conversation with me. He seemed to be very kind and personable.

It wasn't long, however, before I noticed several New Hampshire State troopers and local police officers surrounding the bank. Two of the officers casually walked in and arrested the man. They told me he had passed several bad checks at other banks earlier in the day. One of the officers even showed me a loaded .357 Magnum handgun the would-be thief was carrying. So much for kindness!

George MacDonald wrote, "A man must not choose his neighbor: he must take the neighbor that God sends him. The neighbor is just the man who is next to you at the moment, the man with whom any business has brought you into contact."[82] While we know the parable of the Good Samaritan is a parable about kindness, how then do we show kindness to our neighbors whom God has sent to us at this moment?

We have all heard the words, "How can I ever repay you?" in response to a favor done. Once in a while, someone answers by saying, "No, that won't be necessary. But if you really want to repay me, look for someone else to help; you can pay me back by doing something for another person."

The Good Samaritan story tells us that Jesus spoke of a man in great need. He had been robbed, beaten, and left for dead. Neither the priest nor the Levite showed him kindness. Remember: these people were the upper classes among the Jews. They obviously were neither kind nor merciful. However, the Samaritan was.

We see Jesus exposing the self-righteous pride of many Jews in His day. Pride fueled their unkindness. The Samaritan was simply moved to act with compassion. He bandaged the man's wounds and brought him to an inn to heal. In addition, he paid for the man's expenses.

The following story came from a note a church visitor gave me. It said, "I was hungry, and you formed a humanities club and discussed my hunger. I was imprisoned, and you crept off quietly to your chapel and prayed for my release. I was naked, and, in your mind, you debated the morality of my appearance. I was sick, and you knelt and thanked God for your health. I was homeless, and you preached to me of the spiritual shelter of the love of God. I was lonely, and you left me alone to pray for me. You seem so close to God, but I am still very hungry, and lonely, and cold."

So often, "little deeds of kindness, little words of love help to make earth happy, like the heaven above."[83] While the word *kindness* is not often used in the New Testament, many examples of kindness appear. Before Christ, "the Greeks spoke of things as 'useful', 'serviceable', 'effective'; and of people as 'outgoing', 'useful', and 'benevolent'. In doing so they used the root from which our word 'kindness' is taken. In many New Testament passages we see examples of such 'usefulness' but perhaps no more clearly than in the actions of the Good Samaritan (Luke 10:25–37)."[84]

Some seminary students were once asked to preach on the story of the Good Samaritan. When the hour arrived for their sermons, each one was deliberately delayed en route to class. As the students raced across campus, they encountered a person who pretended to have a heart attack. Ironically, not one of the students stopped to help. After all, they had important sermons to preach! Clearly, followers of Christ can preach powerful sermons to the world when they reflect God's kindness. However, this means showing a Samaritan's kindness to others – not just talking about it.

So what about us? Each time we meet someone in need of God's love, we should live out the parable of the Good Samaritan. We should take the time and trouble to get involved. It might mean helping a neighbor who is struggling financially or perhaps lending a listening ear to someone who is hurting. It may mean sharing the good news of Jesus Christ with someone the Lord brings our way. Or will we be like those religious leaders who quickly passed by on the other side and offered no help?

The old television show, *Leave it to Beaver,* featured a classic hypocrite. His name was Eddie Haskell. Remember him? He seemed to be the kind of guy everyone just loved to hate. On many occasions, he was the one responsible for getting Wally and Beaver into trouble. Eddie would often abuse Beaver's naive allegiance. When Mr. Cleaver entered the room, Eddie would often respond with a line such as "Hello, how are you today, Mr. Cleaver, sir?" Of course, Mr. Cleaver was wise to Eddie and would respond with kindness toward him. After Mr. Cleaver would leave the room Eddie might say something to Beaver like "Hey, what's your old man all bent out of shape for, Beaver?"

We've all heard it said that the best place to find a helping hand is at the end of your own arm. We hear a lot today about Good Samaritan laws. Many years ago,

When eleven-year old Elizabeth Lee reached into a lion cage at an Anchorage amusement park, a 300lb. lioness named Glen grabbed her arm in its teeth. Alaska State Trooper Frank Johnson raced to the rescue, pulled out his pistol and shot the lion in the head. As the lion fell dead, both Johnson and the girl went sprawling; Johnson's gun accidentally went off again, and the girl was wounded in the thigh.

Elizabeth eventually recovered, but she filed a $65,000 damage suit against the trooper, the amusement park and the state of Alaska. The jury decided that the amusement park should pay her $15,000 in damages because the cage was inadequately guarded. It rejected the rest of Elizabeth's claim. Johnson's exoneration was based on Alaska's Good Samaritan statute. Like similar statues in more than forty other states, it holds that one who voluntarily aids a person in distress is not liable for damages unless gross negligence is involved. The English common law traditionally rejected compulsion to save. Instead, it made the rescuer responsible for mishaps caused by his negligence.[85]

On many occasions as I traveled back and forth to seminary in Boston, I saw a white van with the words *Good Samaritan* written on it. Its purpose was to aid drivers whose vehicles had broken down. They provided fuel, antifreeze, a ride, or just a warm, safe place to sit while waiting for a tow. I remember having peace of mind, knowing that help was not far away if I needed it.

Many years ago, I bought a book called *Random Acts of Kindness.* The author made several suggestions explaining how everyday people could show acts of kindness to those around them. I remember using one of them while transporting members of our youth group to a church retreat. I gave the toll booth attendant enough money to pay for the next five cars behind me. As we traveled down the highway, people honked their horns to say thanks or simply gave us a thumbs-up sign. It was a good feeling to show an act of kindness to someone we had never met. More importantly, our youth group learned a valuable lesson in kindness that day.

How many of us have ever traveled alone and wished someone else had come along? Or how many of us have ever had a flat tire and wished someone was there to help?

I recall one story about a woman who used to make a very long drive to visit her parents. While on a particular road in the middle of nowhere, she saw a family whose car was parked on the side of the road with a flat tire. Normally she didn't stop in such situations, but, for some reason, she felt the need to do so that day. The family was very relieved when the woman volunteered to drive them to a gas station several miles down the road to get help. When the gas attendant said he would take the family back to their car, she drove on her way.

After driving a few miles down the same road, she discovered *she* had a flat tire. Since she had never changed a flat tire before, she too became stranded and had no idea what to do. It was not long afterward that a car pulled over to offer help. It happened to be the very same family she stopped to help earlier in the day!

So often, "When we hunger for kindness in our lives, or for love or joy or peace, we are to discover it in the One who is Joy and who is Love and who is Peace and who is Kindness. The gift is contained in the Giver. The two can never be separated. The 'incomparable riches of His grace, expressed in His kindness to us in Christ Jesus' (Ephesians 2:7) is the source of kindness in His people."[86]

Speaking of kindness, there's an old story about a man who was driving along a lonely road one summer day. He saw a car with a flat tire and decided to pull over and offer help. A woman was standing next to her car, looking down in disgust at a flat tire. The man decided to play the Good Samaritan. Soon he became hot, sweaty, and covered with dirt while changing the tire. The woman said to him as he finished, "Please be sure to let the jack down easy now because my husband is sleeping in the back seat of the car!"

Dinah Maria Mulock reminds us to "Keep what is worth keeping and with a breath of kindness, blow the rest away."[87] So why does God expect us to show kindness to others? The reason is found in Luke 6:35 TLB. "Then your reward from heaven will be very great." When we show kindness to others, we imitate God's character in us. In every way we should give as though we are giving to God. Remember: we can never out-give God.

Many times, I have heard the phrase, "You can't help someone uphill without getting closer to the top yourself." I believe it. A colleague told me about a Yale University president who gave the following advice to a former president of Ohio State: "Always be kind to your 'A' and 'B' students because one day one of them will return to your campus as a great professor. Also be kind to your 'C' students because someday one of them will return and build you a two-million-dollar science laboratory!"

Who's been that Good Samaritan in your life? If you had to call someone (outside of your family) at three o'clock in the morning because of a deep personal problem, who would you call? Would you call your pastor, a teacher, a counselor, a close friend, someone with the same problem, or someone you don't even know? To whom have *you* been a Good Samaritan recently?

A man who was down on his luck was panhandling in New York City. As a couple walked by, he said, "May the blessing of the Lord bring you love, joy, and wealth all the days of your life!" As they passed by his outstretched hand without contributing, he yelled, "And *never* catch up with you!" I've heard there are three rules for dealing with all those who approach us: (1) kindness (2) kindness and (3) kindness.

Today, however, we have to be careful. I remember one incident while visiting New York City with my family. A young man approached us with a sign that read: "I am a deaf-mute. Can you spare a few dollars please?" Naturally, we wanted to show God's loving-kindness to those around us, so we made a contribution by putting some money in the tin can he was holding.

Later that day, we saw the same man lying on the grass in Central Park. He was counting all his money and clearly did not appear to be disabled in any way. He was carrying on a very lively conversation with several of his friends. Obviously, he could talk and hear quite well. Unfortunately, these things happen, and so often we feel like we have been taken advantage of.

The book of Romans reminds us that genuine kindness should be our response to God's love. It says, "If someone mistreats you because you are a Christian, don't curse him; pray that God will bless him. When others are happy, be happy with them. If they are sad, share their sorrow" (Romans 12:14 TLB).

I'm sure many of us have learned how to pretend to love others by saying kind words and not hurting their feelings or showing lack of concern. However, God calls us to have real love and to be sincere in our kindness toward others. We help others become better people by using our time, gifts, and talents. While no one person is expected to meet the needs of the whole community, we should at least expect the body of Christ to share in acts of loving-kindness.

Three boy scouts were asked by their scout leader to do an act of kindness one day. Later that afternoon, they returned with news of great success. They told their scout leader they helped an old woman cross a street. He said, "It took all three of you to help an old woman across the street?" "Yes", the boys said. "She didn't want to go!"

"Kindness is something we do for others, not for ourselves, and quite often at the expense of ourselves."[88] A little girl was sent on an errand by her mother. She took much longer than expected to come back. When she returned, the girl's mother demanded an explanation. The little girl explained the reason. On her way, she had met a little friend who was crying because she had broken her doll. "Oh," said the mother, "then you stopped to help her fix her doll?" "Oh no," the little girl said. "I stopped to help her cry!"

Kindness is often a symbol of a loving heart. In his autobiography, *Up from Slavery*, Booker T. Washington "recalled a beautiful memory about his older brother's love. He said the shirts worn on his plantation by the slaves were made of a rough, bristly, inexpensive flax fiber. As a young boy, the garment was so abrasive to his tender, sensitive skin that it caused him a great deal of pain and discomfort. His older brother, moved by his brother's suffering, would wear Booker's new shirts, until they were broken in and smoother to the touch. Booker said it was one of the most striking acts of kindness he had experienced among his fellow slaves."[89]

This certainly is a wonderful illustration and helpful reminder for us to "Bear ye one another's burdens" (Galatians 6:2 KJV). The amazing thing about kindness is the more you use it the more you have. John H. Timmerman adds, "The way we greet each other, talk to each other, do things for each other; these are the starting points for kindness in the family of God."[90]

I've often said to people over the years, inch by inch is a cinch and yard by yard is very hard. We need to hear that "kindness, like peace and joy and love, is a by-product. It is an outcome, not an effort."[91] Oftentimes, kindness pays most when we don't do it for pay.

A teacher asked his students to tell him the meaning of loving-kindness. One little boy stood up and said, "Well, if I was really hungry and someone gave me a slice of bread, that would be kindness. But if they put a little strawberry jam on it, that would be loving-kindness."

Kindness, according to Colossians, should be one of the characteristics of God's people. This passage reminds us, "Therefore, as God's chosen people, holy and dearly loved, clothe yourselves with compassion, kindness, humility, gentleness and patience" (Colossians 3:12).

Here the apostle Paul gives us a strategy to live by every day. He suggests we imitate Christ's compassionate, forgiving attitude, let love guide our lives, let Christ's peace rule in our hearts, always be thankful, keep God's Word in us at all times, and to live as Christ's representatives in the world. A colleague once commented, "One kind act will teach more love of God than a thousand sermons."

It was the great Washington DC socialite and hostess Perle Mesta who, when asked the secret of her success in getting so many rich and famous people to attend her parties, replied, "[It's] all in the greetings and the good-byes. As each guest arrived she met him or her with 'At last you're here!' And as each left she expressed her regrets with: 'I'm sorry you have to leave so soon!'"[92] It's always best to pass kindness on to others.

Stephen Grellet was a French-born Quaker who died in New Jersey in 1855. Grellet would be unknown to the world today except for a few lines that made him immortal. The familiar lines, which have served as an inspiration to so many people, are these: "I shall pass through this world but once. Any good that I can do, or any kindness that I can show to any human being, let me do it now and not defer it. For I shall not pass this way again."[93]

In life, we have to deal with people. They are everywhere: in our homes, our workplaces, our churches, shopping malls, and our favorite vacation spots. People are everywhere! Whether we like it or not, we need people. There are, however, times when we wish we could live without them.

Learning to deal with people is very important today. In many ways, people help us live healthier and happier lives. Certainly Jesus' Sermon on the Mount helps us see the importance of getting along with people by demonstrating loving-kindness.

Once in a while, I still hear the phrase, "putting the cart before the horse." While it's a common phrase, it also reflects a type of shared experience. We all tend to get things mixed up once in a while. We get the cart before the horse and become frustrated about which direction we should take. Perhaps we should ask, "How can we be more kind?" It's been suggested we follow ten simple rules: Go do something for someone else, and repeat it nine more times.

Sometimes we're unkind toward those in our churches. I remember one usher instructing another about the details of proper ushering. He said, "And remember: we have nothing but good, kind Christians in this church until you try to seat someone else in their pew." Unfortunately, this comment is true; I have seen it happen in some of the churches I have served.

How do we act with kindness toward others? How can we put people at ease in our presence and help them feel close to us? Or do we speak harshly of newcomers? Are we threatened by them in some way? Why is it that some churches give a cold shoulder to visitors, making them uncomfortable around us? How do we describe kindness? John H. Timmerman says, "Kindness may be described as standing outside oneself to see and meet the needs of others."[94]

Jesus reminds us, "Whoever serves Me must follow Me; and where I am, My servant also will be. My Father will honor the one who serves Me" (John 12:26). We should always remember that *kindness* is never out of season.

CHAPTER 6

GOODNESS

Mark Twain once wrote, "When I was a boy, I was walking along a street and happened to spy a cart full of watermelons. I was fond of watermelon, so I sneaked quietly up to the cart and snitched one. Then I ran into a nearby alley and sank my teeth into the melon. No sooner had I done so, however, than a strange feeling came over me. Without a moment's hesitation, I made my decision. I walked back to the cart, replaced the melon – and took a ripe one."[95]

One could easily ask whether there can be any good ending to all that is wrong with our world. To me, the book of Job seems to say we can have faith in God's goodness despite our circumstances. Scripture reminds us, "In the land of Uz there lived a man whose name was Job. This man was blameless and upright; he feared God and shunned evil" (Job 1:1).

As we see catastrophes and suffering in the book of Job, we should remember that we live in a fallen world. Good behavior is not always rewarded. Likewise, bad behavior is not always punished. When we see criminals prospering or an innocent child suffering in pain, we say, "That's wrong."

Sin often twists justice and makes our world seem unpredictable and repulsive. The book of Job shows a good man suffering through no apparent fault of his own. Unfortunately, our world is often like that. Job's story, however, doesn't end in hopelessness and despair. Throughout his life, we see that his faith in God is justified even when everything seemed hopeless. Faith, when based on rewards or prosperity, is empty. Faith must be built on confidence in God's ultimate purpose in our lives.

What do you think of when you hear the words *God's goodness?* It's been said that "we may work in darkness, and see no present fruit, but we work for a faithful Master, and through His grace our reward is sure."[96] As Christians, we are "called to state the good news, as Wesley often said, 'plain and home,' that God was in Christ reconciling the world to Himself, that He sent His Son to take the place of the sinner before the judgment of God, that when we trust in Christ we participate in both His death and resurrection, that we can trust that the same goodness of God revealed in Jesus will be present in the world to come, and that God will not give us a trial greater than we can endure."[97]

Psalm 107:1 tells us to "Give thanks to the Lord for He is good." This message should be sung with thanksgiving for all to hear! Billy R. Hearn adds, "God is so good, God is so good, God is so good, He's so good to me!"[98] Goodness has been defined as "becoming in character like God, a Christlike character from which may come exposure or rebuke of sin or evil to please God."[99]

The word *sincere* comes from two Latin words that mean "without wax." Craftsmen of Middle Eastern countries created highly expensive statuettes out of very fine porcelain. Extreme care had to be taken when firing these figurines to keep them from cracking. Dishonest dealers would often buy cracked figurines at much lower prices and then fill the cracks with wax before reselling them. However, honest merchants displayed their uncracked porcelain pieces with signs that read, *sine cera* or without wax.

As followers of Christ, we should be sincere in our goodness toward others, in spite of the circumstances in which we find ourselves. We should, "regard every circumstance, however ungratifying, as among God's good gifts to Him, the expression of a beneficent purpose and, if rightly used, a sure means to His lasting profit."[100]

Through the use of the word *goodness* in Scripture, we see those who have been made righteous in Christ. The root word of *goodness,* according to J.D. Douglas, means "to be upright in character and constitution and beneficial in effect. A study of the Saxon term for deity shows that 'God' was an abbreviation of the word 'good' and literally meant 'the Good One.'"[101]

It's said that "the doctrine of creation also means that nothing made is intrinsically evil. Everything has come from God, and the creation narrative says five times He saw that it was good (Genesis 1:10, 12, 18, 21, 25). Then, when He completed His creation of man, we are told that God saw everything He had made and it was very good."[102]

The word for *good* is the "most comprehensive term used when praising excellence of something. To speak about a good book or good food is to use 'good' in typically nonmoral ways. However, good conveys a moral sense when someone says, 'he is a good man' or 'she did a good deed/work.'"[103]

In his book, *All I Really Need to Know I Learned in Kindergarten*, Robert Fulghum says, "Good people, who are always 'there', can be relied upon in small, important ways. People who teach us, bless us, encourage us, support us, uplift us in daily life. We never tell them. I don't know why, but we don't."[104]

A student once asked his seminary professor, "Does a good beginning and a good ending make a good sermon?" The professor said, "Only if they are close enough together." This reminds me of the story about a church member who dozed off to sleep during the morning service. The preacher said, "Will all who want to go to heaven please stand." All stood except the sleeping parishioner. After they sat down, the pastor continued by saying, "Will all who want to go to the other place please stand." Somebody suddenly dropped a hymnal, and the sleeping man jumped to his feet and stood awkwardly facing the preacher. He said, "Well preacher, I don't know what we're voting for, but it looks like you and I are the only ones for it!"

When we hear the phrase "for goodness sake," I wonder, are we really that surprised? Or, are we just denying God's goodness in those "I don't know" statements? To acknowledge God as good is "the foundation of all biblical thinking about moral goodness. 'Good' in Scripture is not an abstract quality, nor is it a secular human ideal; 'good' means first and foremost what God is, then what He does, creates, commands and gives, and finally what He approves in the lives of His creatures."[105] Goodness, therefore, is "love in action, love with its hand to the plow, love with the burden on its back, love following His footsteps who went about continually doing good."[106]

So what does goodness actually mean? "Specifically the word *agathos* means goodness, uprightness, and generosity. This is how it happens that the translation of the word *agathos* in the story of the rich landholder becomes the word 'generous.' His goodness was expressed in a generous act that did not rest on 'fairness' but on a desire for the other's well being."[107] Often, true goodness is seen flowing from our Christian faith. Therefore, God's goodness requires action on behalf of His people.

A boy ran to his father and said, "I've got a joke you can't guess this time." "What is it?" his father smiled. "Three frogs were sitting on a limb by a pool. One frog decided to jump into the pool. How many frogs were left on the limb?" His father answered, "Well, if one jumped, two would be left." "Nope," said the boy. So his father tried a second time to answer the question. He said, "I see. When one jumped, the others would too, so none would be left." The boy laughed. "No, Dad, you really missed that one. There were three left. Don't you see? The frog only *decided* to jump."

Like the frog, good intentions won't get us into heaven. As Christians, we need to respond in obedient faith. The apostle Paul tells us in the book of Romans that his readers were "full of goodness, filled with all knowledge, able also to admonish one another" (Romans 15:14 KJV). He had total confidence in them.

Their goodness and knowledge had grown to such an extent that they could criticize one another to everyone's benefit. John W. Sanderson adds, "It takes goodness to give beneficial criticism; it takes goodness to receive it and put it to salutary use; and the result of such criticism, thus given and thus received, will be greater goodness within the Christian community."[108] Whenever goodness is exercised, it reveals something about God's Spirit. Often, "goodness, of all dignities and virtues of the mind, is greatest because it is the character of God."[109]

Of all the spiritual fruit, "'goodness' is the one which seems to be more exclusively an attribute of God. Jesus detected superficiality in the young ruler's speech when the latter called Him, 'Good master'. He did not deny that the word applied to Him, but He wanted the young man to see that 'good' in the absolute sense can be applied only to God. So He asked him, 'Why do you call me good? No one is good except God.' A man can be good only in a relative sense."[110]

We've all heard the saying that no news is good news. However, there's a story about a crippled newspaper boy who gave his life to help the world in his own way. Willie Rugh lived in Gary, Indiana. One day he chose to give some skin from his crippled, polo-damaged leg to Ethel Smith, a burn victim, whom he hardly knew. The operation was successful, but soon he developed pneumonia. The doctor told him he wouldn't recover. In a weak voice and a smile on his face, Willie said, "I'm glad I did it, doctor. Please tell her I hope she gets well real soon."

The boy turned his face away as he mumbled, "I guess I'm some good to someone after all."

Newspapers everywhere published the story in 1912. The whole town went into mourning. Public offices and local businesses closed. A band and contingent of police led his body to the cemetery. People contributed large amounts of money to erect a monument in his memory. The mayor proclaimed that Willie's name should be remembered forever.

The word for *good* in the New Testament was used in early times to show that doing good things often brings about a sense of well-being. One of God's faithful missionaries, Allen Gardiner, suffered many physical difficulties and hardships during his service to God. Throughout his life, he was often heard saying, "God gives me strength, but failure will not intimidate me."

In 1851, at the age of fifty-seven, Gardiner died from disease and starvation while serving as a missionary on Picton Island off the southern tip of South America. His diary was found not far from his body. It spoke of hunger, thirst, wounds, and loneliness. The last entry in his diary showed a struggling hand as he tried to write legibly. He wrote, "I am overwhelmed with a sense of God's goodness." It's such a brief message, and yet there are no words of complaint, no whining or grumbling about the circumstances in which he found himself. There was only praise for God's goodness.

God reminds us that, in spite of evil, He's still working out His good purposes. The Bible says, "As far as I am concerned, God turned into good what you meant for evil, for He brought me to this high position I have today so that I could save the lives of many people" (Genesis 50:20 TLB). When Joseph became a slave, Jacob thought he was dead and wept in despair (Genesis 37:30). Eventually God's plan allowed Jacob to regain his son and grandchildren.

We should remember that our circumstances are never so difficult that we are beyond God's help. Jacob not only regained his son but Job got a new family (Job 42:10–17). Mary regained her brother, Lazarus (John 11:1–44). We should never feel hopeless or in despair when we belong to our loving God. He can bring good out of every hopeless situation.

Joseph's experiences helped him understand that God can bring good out of every evil situation when we trust Him. The question is do we trust God enough to wait patiently for Him while He brings good out of bad situations? We should trust God because, as Joseph learned, He overrides our evil intentions; this in turn brings about His intended results.

Abraham Lincoln trusted God's goodness. According to James Hastings,

> Joseph R. Sizoo, one-time pastor of the New York Avenue Presbyterian Church in Washington which Abraham Lincoln often attended, says he will never forget the day he held in his hands for the first time the Bible of Abraham Lincoln. It was the Bible from which Lincoln's mother had read to him as a child. She had taught him to commit to memory many of its passages. It was the only possession Lincoln carried from Pigeon Creek to the Sangamon River. And book in my hand, I wondered where it would fall open. It opened to a page which was thumb-marked and which he must have read many times. It was the thirty-seventh Psalm, 'Fret not thyself because of evildoers ... Rest in the Lord, and wait patiently for him' (Psalm 37:1, 7 KJV).[111]

When God is in control of our lives, we can overcome evil with good.

After a family returned home from a Sunday morning service, the father criticized the pastor's sermon. The daughter thought the choir's singing was off key, and the mother thought the organist played badly. The subject had to be changed when their small son said, "But it was a good show for a nickel, don't you think, Dad?"

I wonder sometimes if the goodness we show toward others is just a 'put-on' when we are around certain people and yet quite different when they are not around. God has a way to "create something good, because He is goodness itself. But humans have another capacity; to do good or evil."[112]

So often, we hear the old expression, "A bad tree doesn't yield good apples." I believe the following story illustrates this thought. I understand that "Max Jukes lived in New York. He did not believe in Christ or in Christian training. He refused to take his children to church, even when they asked to go. He has had 1,026 descendants; 300 were sent to prison for an average term of thirteen years; 190 were public prostitutes, 680 were admitted alcoholics. His family, thus far, has cost the state in excess of $420,000. They made no contribution to society."[113]

On the other hand, "Jonathan Edwards lived in the same state, at the same time as Jukes. He loved the Lord and saw that his children were in church every Sunday, as he served the Lord to the best of his ability. He has had 929 descendants, and of these 430 were ministers; 86 became university professors; 13 became university presidents; 75 authored good books; 7 were elected to the United States Congress. One was vice president of his nation. His family never cost the state one cent but has contributed immeasurably to the life of plenty in this land today."[114]

I believe every person has the capacity both for good and evil. The following story illustrates this point. A lighthouse keeper worked on a rocky stretch of coastline. He had just received his new supply of oil for the month to keep the light burning. He had frequent guests, being so close to shore. On one particular night, a woman from town begged him for some oil to keep her family warm. The next day, an old man asked for some oil to use in his lamp. Still another person needed some to lubricate a wheel for his water pump. Since all the requests seemed legitimate, the lighthouse keeper granted all their requests.

Toward the end of the month, however, he noticed that his supply of oil was very low. Soon, it was all gone, and the beacon light went out. That night, several ships wrecked, and many lives were lost. When the authorities investigated, the man was very remorseful. Their reply was, "You were given the oil for one purpose – to keep that light burning!"

The Psalmist writes, "How abundant are the good things that you have stored up for those who fear you, that you bestow in the sight of all, on those who take refuge in you" (Psalm 31:19). Richard Roberts adds, "There are no days when God's fountain does not flow."[115]

Speaking of the flow of goodness, I heard the following story in a restaurant. A motorist, after getting stuck in a muddy road, paid a passing farmer fifty dollars to pull him out with his tractor. Once back on dry ground, he said to the farmer, "At those prices, I would think you'd be pulling people out of the mud all day and night!" The farmer said, "I can't, because at night I haul water for the hole!"

Stephen F. Bayne states, "Unique in your wickedness or unique in your goodness – they come too much the same thing in the end.

The one thing man cannot abide is just being part of humanity. We spend our lives looking over our shoulders at our neighbors to be sure that we are a little bit ahead of them, a little more knowing, a little better established in goodness, a little more honest in our sin."[116] Steven Winward adds, "The Hebrew word for good (tob) is used not only of the ethically and morally good but also of that which is attractive, pleasant and beautiful."[117]

We often hear these polite pleasantries: it's good to see you, good gracious, good for you, good memories, good enough, good food, good times, goodness sake or have a good day. We've all heard people described as being good natured, good humored, good hearted, good to me, or having good intentions. On the other hand, phrases like good for nothing, good riddance, good-bye, or Good Friday can take on different meanings.

Even when people mean well, they sometimes create more problems than they solve. One young pastor, while spreading the good news, was making hospital rounds for the first time. Visiting an elderly parishioner, he walked in and plopped himself down on the side of her bed. He began aggressively questioning her about her surgery. Before leaving, he asked, "Is there anything else I can do for you?" The sweet old lady replied, "Well, if you don't mind, would you please take your foot off my oxygen hose?"

In his book, *The Tree of Life: Plain Sermons on the Fruit of the Spirit*, Harry J. Wilmot-Buxton states, "Those who never do any good in the world, and try to keep their religion entirely to themselves, are like the miser who buries his coins in the earth. He has a treasure but it is useless to him because it does not circulate from hand to hand. My brethren, Christianity is worthless unless we spend it by doing good to our fellow men. That is working for Christ. Whenever we try to help a fellowman we are ministering unto the Lord Jesus."[118]

I've heard it said that a good heart is better than all the heads in the world. Have you heard about the two moving men who were struggling with a big crate in a doorway? They pushed and pulled until both were completely exhausted. Finally, the man on the outside said, "We might as well give up. We'll never get this thing in." The man on the inside yelled back, "What do you mean, get it in? I thought we were trying to get it out!" As Christians, I wonder if we're like that – some pushing one way and others pushing another way. There's nothing like cooperation to move us in the same direction to get a job done.

Sometimes we ask, "What is happening to me? Why does this happen? What hope have I for the future? What should I think about this? What should I do? Why should I do it?" These are natural questions about the constant mystery of good and evil. God wants us to have answers to these questions, and to help others find them. However, sometimes the answers lie in learning what questions to ask and the right way to ask them.

When creation was completed, Genesis 1:31 says, "God saw all that He made, and it was very good." Scripture also reminds us, "For everything God created is good, and nothing is to be rejected if it is received with thanksgiving" (1 Timothy 4:4). Jesus said we are to "Do good to those who hate you" (Luke 6:27 TLB).

As humans, we are "much too puny to do it all, but we do have the help of a divine Savior in our effort. We are at work to redeem the earth with the help of Jesus, but to do so we must do good."[119] We're fortunate God allows U-turns in our lives. Thomas Jefferson once suggested the following ten rules for the good life:

1. Never put off till tomorrow what you can do today.
2. Never trouble another for what you can do yourself.
3. Never spend your money before you have it.
4. Never buy what you do not want because it is cheap; it will be dear to you.
5. Pride costs us more than hunger, thirst and cold.
6. Never repent of having eaten too little.
7. Nothing is troublesome that we do willingly.
8. Don't let the evils, which have never happened, cost you pain.
9. Always take things by their smooth handle.
10. When angry, count to ten before you speak; if very angry, count to one hundred.[120]

What is the source of goodness? Jesus said, "Only God is truly good" (Mark 10:18 TLB). God alone represents complete goodness. At times, however, it seems God created this good world, and His creation wants to destroy it. Even though there is evil in the world, we are called to "Hate the evil, and love the good, and establish judgment in the gate" (Amos 5:15 KJV).

A small child wrote the following prayer: "Dear God, make all the bad people good, and make all the good people nice." We should remember that "God is not content with our doing what is right some of the time. He wants us to do what is right all the time."[121] We should take encouragement from God's Word to do good because He is the source of all goodness. Additionally, "our good deeds are in warfare against evil. We represent Christ on this earth and we also represent His warfare against evil."[122]

Jesus urges us to be like His Father. "But love your enemies, do good to them, and lend to them without expecting to get anything back. Then your reward will be great, and you will be children of the Most High" (Luke 6:35). Don't you think our world would be a better and happier place to live in if we could all just spread around a little more goodness?

Out of the goodness of his heart a man once sent a letter to the IRS. It read, "Dear Sir: Last year, when I filed my income tax return, I deliberately misrepresented my income. Now I cannot sleep. Enclosed is a check for $150 for taxes. If I still cannot sleep, I will send you the rest."

Jesus believed that our goodness should be contagious. Remember those TV ads aimed at USMC recruits? They said, "We need a few good men." Our Lord expects the same from us because our goodness should reflect the God we serve.

Many years ago, Joseph Stowell, a consultant to some of the largest United States companies, was speaking about quality control and consumer relations issues. One man asked him to compare ministry as a form of human quality control. He basically said, "Quality control is not concerned about the product but with the process." He added, "If the process is right, the product is always guaranteed." It's interesting how relevant this is to Christianity today. Sometimes we're more concerned about the product of our faith than with the process.

But, not all charity has a good result. Two girls got onto a crowded bus. One of them whispered to the other, "Watch me embarrass that man over there into giving me his seat." Pushing her way through the crowd, she turned all her charms on a man who looked like he might embarrass easily. She politely said, "Hello, Mr. Wilson. It's so good to see you today! I'm so tired."

The old man looked up at the girl, and although he had never seen her before, he got up and pleasantly said, "Please sit down, Mary, my girl. It's not often I see you on washday. No wonder you're so tired. Being pregnant isn't easy. By the way, don't deliver the wash until Thursday. My wife is going to the district attorney's office to see whether or not she can get your husband out of jail." Sometimes goodness demands respect.

The old hymn, *"Rescue the Perishing,"* expresses the potential good that can come from encouraging others to profess their Christian faith. The words say, "Down in the human heart, crushed by the tempter, feelings lie buried that grace can restore. Touched by a loving hand, wakened by kindness, chords that were broken will vibrate once more."[123] Every Christian should have the assurance that goodness will overcome evil in the end.

The gospel of John reveals that God's ability to do 'good' is not limited by our own understanding. The Bible says, "When He heard this, Jesus said, 'This sickness will not end in death. No, it is for God's glory so that God's Son may be glorified through it'" (John 11:4).

When Martha and Mary's brother became ill, what did they do? They simply turned to Jesus for help. They believed Jesus had the ability to heal because they had seen His miracles before. God's Word can still change lives today. Miracles continue to happen. When we need extraordinary help, Jesus is there to offer extraordinary resources. We should never hesitate to ask Jesus for help in our lives.

As Christians, we must believe God can bring good out of any bad situation (Genesis 50:20). Unfortunately, many people complain or blame God rather than seeing their problems as opportunities to praise and honor Him. Remember: God sees all we do in building up His kingdom and even rewards us for it!

A little boy was helping his father prepare a new garden for planting and decided to pull out an old cornstalk. With excitement in his voice, he told his dad, "I pulled out this cornstalk all by myself!" His father said, "Yes, you did, son; you're a strong boy!" The little boy said, "Yes, and the whole world was pulling at the other end!" How many times have we felt the same way in our lives, when the whole world seems to be tugging on us in difficult times?

Paul Harvey once said, "Too many Christians are no longer fishers of men but keepers of the aquarium." A woman who was expecting extra guests for dinner needed to buy more food. She stopped by a small grocery store meat counter and asked the clerk for a large chicken. He reached down into the freezer and grabbed the last chicken he had. As he put it on the scale, he said, "This one weighs four pounds ma'am." The woman said, "That will not be enough. Don't you have a bigger one?"

The clerk put the chicken back into the freezer, pretended to search through the ice for another one, and then brought out the same chicken. Placing in on the scale once again, he applied pressure from his finger. With a smile, he said, "Ah, this one weighs six pounds!" The woman replied with a frown, "I'm just not sure. I'll tell you what. Wrap them both up for me!" Everyone should remember that goodness is so simple. We should live for others and take advantage of no one.

A desert wanderer found a spring of cool fresh water. It was so pure he decided to bring some to his king. Barely satisfying his own thirst, he filled a leather bottle and carried it many days in the desert sun before reaching the palace. He laid his offering at the feet of his noble king. Over time, however, the water had become stale in the old container. But the king wouldn't let his faithful subject think his gift was unfit to drink. He tasted it with gratitude as he sent his loyal servant away. After the servant left, others sampled it and were surprised the king had pretended to enjoy it. He said, "It wasn't the water I tasted but the love that prompted his offering."

Oftentimes, our service is seen only through its imperfections, but the Lord looks at our motives and says, "It is good." Scripture says, "As cold waters to a thirsty soul, so is good news from a far country" (Proverbs 25:25 KJV). We should let no opportunity slip away by "showing gentleness and goodness. Life is short, but God gives you many opportunities of usefulness; each day brings them; neglect them not, for the account is heavy."[124]

The Old Testament tells us, "Whatever your hand finds to do, do it with all your might" (Ecclesiastes 9:10). When it comes to opportunities for service, Jesus says to "give, and it will be given to you. A good measure, pressed down, shaken together and running over, will be poured into your lap. For with the measure you use, it will be measured to you" (Luke 6:38). He adds, "It is more blessed to give then to receive" (Acts 20:35 TLB).

One could easily ask, "What does generosity have to do with goodness?" Both mean the same word, *agatho*, in the New Testament Greek. Imagine what it would be like if God withdrew all His goodness and blessings from us. It was often said of Victor Hugo, "The only thing to which he had learnt to bend the knee was goodness."[125]

On a beautiful, sunny fall day, I decided to climb Chocorua Mountain in northern New Hampshire. I just wanted to get away by myself. I needed to renew my spirit and absorb God's goodness in my soul once again. I wanted to surround myself with His wonderful creation. Everything looked so clear from the top. It truly was a mountain-top experience. I felt like I was on top of the world again!

After soaking up some of those sunny rays, I decided to make my way back down the mountain. As I did, I passed by someone I recognized. So often, we think we'll be all alone in those mountaintop experiences until we recognize we're really never alone in God's presence. So I said, "Hi, I think I know you from some place!" He turned and said, "Yes, let me think where." We finally figured it out. We had worshipped in the same church together many years ago. So I asked him how everything was going. He said, "Just fine." I replied, "That's good!"

As we were leaving each other, he turned around and said, "Well, things aren't so good after all." We sat and talked for some time on Mount Chocorua that day. He told me his wife had recently divorced him, and that his only son had committed suicide the night before. I learned that, even in the midst of overwhelming sorrow and despair, this man – like Job – still held to a faith that believed in God's abundant goodness.

While I didn't completely understand why our paths crossed that particular day, I do believe God's ability to do good through His people is certainly not limited by our own understanding. No matter what vocation we are called to, we are still 'full-time' Christians. I agree that it's "not only the Christian's presence that should make this a better world to live in, it is also his money, effort, time, and abilities dedicated to the amelioration of his neighbors' conditions and to showing them the true goodness of God."[126]

One Sunday, an usher showed concern for a person searching for something beneath his pew. He asked, "May I help you, sir?" The man replied, "I lost my caramel." The usher said, "Oh, I thought it was something important." The old man said, "Yes, it is. My *teeth* are in it!"

Scripture, whether directly or indirectly, speaks volumes about God's goodness. It's something we can literally get our teeth into! When we do, it has real sticking power. Two examples of good people from the book of Acts stand out here. The first is Barnabas (Acts 11:24). He was generous with his possessions and was happy to see others grow in their faith without becoming jealous. The other good person we hear little about is Dorcas (Acts 9:36), who was generous in good works and deeds.

Thinking of good deeds, there's a story about a man who noticed a woman moving her car back and forth in a tight parking space. Being helpful, he stopped to offer his assistance. He guided how she should turn the wheel and when to go forward and when to back up. After a few minutes, with his expertise, her vehicle was parked close to the curb. He said, "There you are. Snug as a bug in a rug!" She replied, "I know, sir, and I appreciate your help. But I wasn't trying to park it. I was trying to get out."

We should note that,

> The fruit of goodness must be understood above all as 'doing the right thing.' Goodness has purpose and authority behind it. In fact, to some people it may not even look like good. It is biblically good, for example, to discipline our children, but it may not seem good to them. Goodness may even be doing the unpopular thing, not to please humans but to please God. We may receive no praise from others when we do good – active, committed good – but as Proverbs 12:20 points out, 'Those who plan good have joy.' This joy that is the result of the fruit of goodness comes from the knowledge that in doing good we do the will of the Lord, even when that doing is unpopular, even when it meets with the scorn of others.'[127]

I am sure Solomon thought this when he wrote, "The faithless will be fully repaid for their ways, and the good rewarded for theirs" (Proverbs 14:14). While both Testaments clearly link true goodness with God, the Psalmist assures us that, "those who seek the Lord lack no good thing" (Psalm 34:10). In addition, the Bible sees God as the "only One who is good" (Matthew 19:17) and knows Him as the source and giver of "every good and perfect gift" (James 1:17). All goodness is on loan to us; however, God is the actual owner.

Ben Franklin once wrote, "When you are good to others, you are best to yourself."[128] God is involved in all aspects of our lives. He wants to bring good to everyone. The apostle Paul adds, "And we know that in all things God works for the good of those who love Him, who have been called according to His purpose" (Romans 8:28).

It's clear that "God works out all things – not just isolated incidents – for our good. This does not mean that all that happens to us is good. Evil is prevalent in our fallen world, but God is able to turn it around for our long-range good."[129]

Often people ask, "Why do bad things happen to good people?" In his book, *The Billy Graham Christian Worker's Handbook*, Graham asks if God is all good and powerful, then why do innocent people suffer? He writes, "Here we have to admit our partial ignorance. We do not have the full explanation of the origin and problem of evil because God has chosen to reveal only a part to us. God created the universe perfect; mankind, through free will, chose to disobey. Evil came into the universe through man's disobedience. Because mankind disobeyed and broke God's law, evil pervades the universe."[130]

God wants to fulfill His purpose in and through us. However, this promise is not for everyone. It's for those who love God and accept His plan for their lives. The Holy Spirit *calls* us to receive Jesus Christ as Lord and Savior. With new lives in Christ, we trust God's way and not the ways of this world. Our treasure and refuge are in heaven, not on earth. Believing this helps us accept life's suffering and pain, knowing that God is always with us.

A tightwad was looking for a gift for his friend. Everything was too expensive except for a glass vase that was chipped and inexpensive to buy. He asked the store to send it, hoping his friend would think it had been broken in shipment. Shortly afterward, he received the following note: "Thanks for the vase. It was so thoughtful of you to wrap each piece separately." We should always consider that "true goodness is not merely impulsive, but rational and considerate."[131]

Jesus often taught that our greatest pleasures in life come from doing good deeds in secret. We're not to look for rewards in return. This isn't a call for us to be part-time do-gooders either. We should do good things for others in all circumstances. Our model should be to always imitate Jesus Himself. The world needs more 'full-time' do-gooders, remembering that doing good works is characteristic of the God we serve.

Both the Old and New Testaments "authorize God's faithful people to rest assured that in God's good time everything that is truly good for them will be made theirs."[132] The apostle Paul said we are re-created "to be like God" (Ephesians 4:24). In other words, just as we were originally created in His image and after His likeness, so we are to model our new lives on God. Keep in mind, however, God's goodness is not automatic. It takes determination and work.

A little girl was sent to her room as punishment. After a while, she went back downstairs in a happier mood. "Well, Mom," she said, "I've thought things over, and I prayed." Her mother said, "That's wonderful. So now you can be a good little girl, right?" She replied, "Oh, I didn't pray to be good. I just asked God to help you put up with me!" At times, it seems this is exactly what we expect from others. We want them to simply put up with us. However, God's goodness is meant to be given away.

One morning, four high school boys were late to their class because they had overslept. When they finally came to class, they explained to their teacher that they'd had a flat tire. Sympathetically, the teacher smiled and said it was too bad because they missed a test that morning. Out of the goodness of her heart, she decided to let them make it up. She gave each of the boys a piece of paper and pencil and then asked them go to a different corner of the room. She told them they would pass if they could answer just one question: which tire was flat?

A reoccurring theme in the Bible suggests we are called to be recipients of God's goodness *and* to be givers. The Bible stresses a higher calling for God's people. We are to bear fruit through good works (Colossians 1:10). We should eagerly seek to do good (1 Thessalonians 5:15; Titus 3:14). Our goodness should be directed toward everyone and not just to those in the household of faith (Galatians 6:6, 10; Romans 15:2).

The people of God should continually seek out this higher calling of God's goodness. At a county fair, a man released a big group of balloons into the air. A little boy turned to his dad and asked, "Why are the red balloons flying higher than the yellow ones?" His father replied, "It's not about the color on the outside; it's about what's inside the balloons that makes the difference." Like us, what's on the inside affects how we grow to new heights in our spiritual lives. So often, becoming gentle on the inside produces goodness on the outside. Goodness is about God's love in action.

I love the words, "God is so good; He's so good to me." But how can we do good things for others? Where can we do what's good around us? How can we make a difference in someone else's life? Will our influence count toward bringing about good results? We should always remember that our strength to do what's good comes not from ourselves but from the God we serve. Faith and courage to do good, can reassure our confidence in Jesus' heavenly promise, "Well done, good and faithful servant" (Matthew 25:21).

Two preachers who didn't get along well met on a street. One of them said, "I heard you speak the other night and recognized that sermon; you preached it fourteen years ago." Shocked, the other preacher yelled back, "I heard you speak just three weeks ago, and I can't remember a word you said!" Here's the lesson. Our lives should be like good sermons. They should convey messages that leave lasting impressions. They should motivate listeners to godly living, to be "good and faithful servants" of God's goodness.

First Corinthians says, "Therefore, my dear brothers and sisters, stand firm. Let nothing move you. Always give yourselves fully to the work of the Lord, because you know that your labor in the Lord is not in vain" (Corinthians 15:58). Sometimes people hesitate in doing good works for others because they don't see the immediate results or benefits from their labors. As Christians, we should remember that our ultimate victory is always in Christ Jesus. We shouldn't become discouraged in the process but always strive to do what's good with eternal results in mind.

Jesus was always doing good works for others. It's a message everyone needs to hear. In that old hymn, *Good Christian Friends Rejoice,* written by John Mason Neale, we sing, "Good Christian friends, rejoice with heart and soul and voice; give ye heed to what we say: News, News! Jesus Christ is born today! Jesus Christ was born to save!"[133] Yes, the *goodness* of God is found by sharing the good news that "Jesus Christ was born to save."

CHAPTER 7

FAITHFULNESS

There's an old story about a man of faith who refuses to leave his home during a flood. When the police come by and advise him to move to higher ground, he says, "God will save me." As the water rises, rescue workers in a boat come by and ask him if he wants to be evacuated. He replies, "God will save me." While sitting on his roof to avoid the rising waters, he refuses help again, this time from a helicopter hovering from above. Finally, the man drowns and goes to heaven. He asks God, "Why didn't you save me?" God said, "What do you mean? I sent a policeman, a boat, and a helicopter!"

What are some examples of faithfulness found in the Bible? The book of Lamentations tells us that even in the midst of great despair Jeremiah clung to God's faithfulness. It says, "Because of the Lord's great love we are not consumed, for His compassion never fails. They are new every morning; great is Your faithfulness" (Lamentations 3:22–23).

Jeremiah saw a ray of hope in all the sin and sorrow surrounding him. From personal experience, he knew about God's faithfulness. God said that punishment would follow disobedience, and it did. He promised restoration and blessing in the future, and Jeremiah knew that too.

Trusting in God's faithfulness day and night gives us confidence in His future promises. God eagerly responds when we ask for help. Sometimes we think there's sin in our lives God won't forgive. However, God's steadfast love and mercy are greater than any sin; He promises us forgiveness.

That wonderful hymn, *"Great Is Thy Faithfulness,"* written by Thomas Chisholm, reminds us of God's hope and promise: "Great is Thy faithfulness, O God my Father; there is no shadow of turning with Thee. Thou changest not, Thy compassions, they fail not; as Thou hast been, Thou forever wilt be. Great is Thy faithfulness! Great is Thy faithfulness! Morning by morning new mercies I see. All I have needed Thy hand hath provided. Great is Thy faithfulness, Lord, unto me!"[134]

The intentional use of exclamation points in this hymn helps us better understand the observation Jay Kesler makes in his book, *Family Forum*. He says, "Faith believes that God is in control; that He made the world, that He can handle any problem we might raise. Faith says, 'Bring on all corners. Let's put them in the arena and wrestle with them. I'm not afraid, because I know God will come out on top!' God protects me."[135]

Dwight Lyman Moody once said there are three kinds of faith in Christ. There is a "struggling faith, like a man in deep water desperately swimming; a clinging faith, like a man hanging to the side of a boat; and a resting faith, like a man safely within the boat (and able to reach out with a hand to help someone else get in)."[136]

Some Christians seem so afraid of failure that they become standoffish, overly cautious and uninvolved in life. They follow a policy of guarded living, holding back time, talents and treasure from God's service. Their motto seems to be to keep from failing, just don't try! However, those who are willing to make mistakes and risk failure are often the ones who ultimately accomplish great things. Instead of being filled with fear, they step forward in faith.

Problems can be challenges, even though they may not all get solved. Some people courageously live with that reality rather than fear failure in their accomplishments. People who accomplish much in life often make many mistakes along the way. However, they never make that one big mistake of doing nothing at all.

My junior high school years were a time of many changes. Before going to school, I used Vitalis to grease my hair. The more I poured on, the better my hair withstood the sometimes harsh weather conditions of New England. The wind could blow a hundred miles an hour, and not a single hair would move, especially when the temperatures were freezing outside. My hair would just freeze in place.

One day, however, I ran out of Vitalis. Frantically, I decided to use some of my older brother's stash, but I couldn't find any. I thought to myself, *What am I going to do now?* After all, I had to put something in my hair before going to school. So I used some shampoo. Everything went well until I started on my way back home. Yes, it rained and my head was full of soapsuds! Instead of putting my trust in a proven product, I put my faith in a bottle of shampoo. What a mistake! On the brighter side, I sure smelled clean that day!

The Bible reminds us, "Now faith is confidence in what we hope for and assurance about what we do not see" (Hebrews 11:1). St. Augustine wrote, "Faith is to believe what we do not see, and the reward of this faith is to see what we believe. This living faith must be cultivated in our lives as believers."[137] Sometimes this means running into obstacles that test our faith.

Did you know that a dense fog covering seven city blocks to a depth of one hundred feet would equal less than a glass of water? Compare this to all the things we worry about today. What if we could see all our problems for what they really are – in their true sizes and shapes? If all the things we worry about the most today were reduced to their true size, perhaps they'd all fit into one glass of water!

We don't always feel God's presence, but that's when we're tested the most. It's then we need to walk with total faith. This is certainly true of the doubting Thomas (John 20:27–29). This contrast of faith and doubt is seen in the following poem:

"Faith and Doubt"

Doubt sees the obstacles,
Faith sees the way!
Doubt sees the darkest night.
Faith sees the day!
Doubt dreads to take a step
Faith soars on high!
Doubt questions, "Who believes?"
Faith answers, "I!"[138]

Christians should be "awake and sober, armed with the breastplate of faith and love and helmeted with hope."[139] While the Old Testament Hebrew word for faith is used only twice, "we should not, however, conclude from the rarity of the word that faith is unimportant in the OT, for the idea, if not the word, is frequent. It is usually expressed by verbs such as 'believe', 'trust' or 'hope', and such abound."[140]

The book of Psalms illustrates this. It says, "Vindicate me, Lord, for I have led a blameless life; I have trusted in the Lord and have not faltered. Test me, Lord, and try me, examine my heart and my mind; for I have always been mindful of your unfailing love and have lived in reliance on your faithfulness" (Psalm 26:1-3).

The New Testament gives great importance to the word *faith*. The "Greek noun *pistis* and the verb *pisteu* both occur more than 240 times, while the adjective *pistos* is found 67 times."[141] These words, in a literal sense, mean, to place ourselves in Christ.

This emphasis on faith should be seen in the context of God's saving work in Christ. God's Son, the Savior of the world, is central to the New Testament. Jesus died on the cross at Calvary to bring salvation to all people. Faith helps us develop the Christian attitude of not relying on our own efforts or deeds for salvation.

When the Philippian jailer asked, "Sirs, what must I do to be saved?" Paul and Silas replied, "Believe in the Lord Jesus, and you will be saved – you and your household" (Acts 16:30–31). Jesus said believers "shall not perish but have eternal life" (John 3:16 TLB). Faith in Christ leads to salvation. Clearly, we see a connection between faithfulness and our attitude toward God.

There's a story about a tourist who came too close to the edge of the Grand Canyon and fell over. He began clawing and scratching at the side of the cliff to save himself. Out of sight and just before he fell into the canyon below, he grabbed hold of a scrubby bush and frantically held on with both hands.

Filled with fear, he called out to heaven, "Is anyone up there?" A calm, powerful voice said, "Yes, this is the Lord." The man pleaded, "Can you help me, Lord?" Again, the voice replied, "Yes, how can I help you?" "I fell over a cliff, and I'm hanging from a branch that's about to break! Please help me!" The Lord said, "Do you believe?" "Yes, yes, Lord, I believe!" "Do you have faith?" "Yes, yes. I have strong faith!" The Lord said, "Let go of the branch." After a brief pause, the man yelled out, "Is anyone *else* up there?"

Our faithfulness to God should be seen as "being trustworthy, dependable, or reliable in daily life with others and the Lord."[142] The book of Peter reminds us,

> In all this you greatly rejoice, though now for a little while you may have had to suffer grief in all kinds of trials. These have come so that your faith – of greater worth than gold, which

perishes even though refined by fire – may result in praise, glory and honor when Jesus Christ is revealed. Though you have not seen Him, you love Him; and even though you do not see Him now, you believe in Him and are filled with an inexpressible and glorious joy, for you are receiving the end result of your faith, the salvation of your souls.

—1 Peter. 1:6–9

"Faith is the bird that feels the light and sings to greet the dawn while it is still dark."[143] Even today, whenever I see a rainbow, I am reminded of the story of Noah and of his great faith, which saved his family from destruction. The book of Hebrews says, "By faith Noah, when warned about things not yet seen, in holy fear built an ark to save his family" (Hebrews 11:7).

Many in the Bible put their faith on the line for God. There's a certain element of risk involved in faith. None, however, is as impressive as Jesus' life and example. He put His faith on the line several times, especially in the Garden of Gethsemane. Jesus put His faith on the line to do God's will, even if it meant dying on a cross. Where Adam and Eve failed in the Garden of Eden, Jesus succeeded in the Garden of Gethsemane. Our Lord exemplified faithfulness in doing the work of the kingdom of God.

Have you ever heard the unusual account of how news of the battle of Waterloo reached England? A ship carried the word first to the southern coast. From there, it was relayed by signal flags to London. When the report reached Winchester, the flags on the cathedral began to spell out "Wellington defeated." But before the message could be completed, a heavy fog moved in. Gloom filled the hearts of many people as the fragmented news spread throughout the surrounding countryside. However, when the fog began to lift, it became clear the signals of Winchester Cathedral had really spelled out this triumphant message: "Wellington defeated the enemy!"

Too often, we allow our futures to be seen through eyes focused on the present moment. We have a tendency to become so absorbed by our current problems we forget God's faithfulness in the past. I find it interesting that three little words, *I doubt it,* have become a catchphrase these days. We've become a generation of question marks. It's not that people find believing in God difficult, but people tend to choose belief in all kinds of things other than God.

There's a story James S. Hewett includes in *Illustrations Unlimited*. It's about a victim of the Holocaust who left a message for the whole world to see. It reads, "Sweeping across Germany at the end of World War II, Allied forces searched farms and houses looking for snipers. At one abandoned house, almost a heap of rubble, searchers with flashlights found their way to the basement. There, on the crumbling wall, a victim of the Holocaust had scratched a Star of David. And beneath it, in rough lettering, the message: 'I believe in the sun – even when it does not shine; I believe in love – even when it is not shown; I believe in God – even when He does not speak.'"[144]

Billy Graham wrote, "Faith will manifest itself in three ways: in doctrine, worship, and fellowship. It will manifest itself in morality in the way we live and behave. The Bible also teaches that faith does not end with trust in Christ for our salvation. Faith continues! Faith grows! It may be weak at first, but it will become stronger as we begin to read the Bible, pray, go to church, and experience God's faithfulness in our Christian life."[145] Faith means placing our trust completely in God.

There's a story about an old European monastery, built high on a cliff five hundred feet high. Visitors to the monastery could only reach the top by being pulled up in a big basket with an old ragged rope. Halfway up, a passenger once nervously asked, "How often do you change the rope?" The monk in charge replied, "Whenever the old one breaks."

We know the mountains we climb in life are not all physical. Often, "In the case of physical mountains it is not for us to move here what God has planted there. Our faith is not to disrupt the order of God's creation. But there may very well be a figurative mountain in our lives that we by faith can ask God to move and it will be moved. By removing such a figurative mountain, God's order may be restored."[146]

The real question is what mountain in *your* life needs to be moved or removed through faith? God's Spirit produces this fruit of faith. It doesn't come as a result of our own efforts but from God.

A grandmother named Taw Bow lived in Thailand. She was small in stature and bent over with age; her fingers were crippled with arthritis. She often stood silently to one side. Her name, translated into English, meant "always." Despite her physical appearance, Grandma

Always inspired her missionary friends and fellow Thai Christians with her faithfulness.

A widow over ninety, she lived as a servant in a Thai home. Every Sunday she walked two miles to church. Out of her income of five cents a day, she regularly gave one day's wage to the Lord every week. Whenever her friends drove her home from church, she got out and bowed her head in grateful prayer for their work in Christ. The missionaries fondly remembered the humble faithfulness of Grandma Always. I wonder what would happen if her example was followed in our local churches and communities.

I was impressed by Old Faithful in Yellowstone National Park during a visit several years ago. I learned that, unlike other geysers, Old Faithful gets its name from the fact that it follows a dependable time schedule. I was told that a stream of boiling water shoots into the air over 170 feet once every sixty-five minutes. Christians everywhere should have this same dependable schedule of faithfulness in their daily devotional lives.

Throughout biblical history, God has always had a remnant of faithful followers. In 1 Kings, Elijah replies, "I have been very zealous for the Lord God Almighty. The Israelites have rejected your covenant, torn down your altars, and put your prophets to death with the sword. I am the only one left, and now they are trying to kill me too" (Kings 19:10).

Elijah thought he was the only one left who was still faithful to God. While he experienced victory at Mount Carmel, Elijah had to run for his life. He was lonely and discouraged. Elijah seemed to forget that others remained faithful as well during this time.

Sometimes we think we're the only ones remaining faithful in doing God's work. We should stop feeling sorry for ourselves because self-pity oftentimes takes away from the good we do. We should rest assured that, even though we may not know them, there are others who still faithfully fulfill God's purpose through their Christian service. Like the man in Canada who rang the church bell every Sunday for fifty years, one can certainly say he represents a long record of faithful service.

A pastor was speaking to his parishioners on the relationship between fact and faith. He said, "That you are sitting before me in this church is a fact. That I'm standing here, speaking from this pulpit, is a fact. But to believe anyone is listening to me is pure faith!" It's amazing to think that an acorn's purpose is to one day turn into a huge oak. However, we know not all acorns turn into healthy trees!

Outside the cemetery of Greyfriars Churchyard in Edinburgh, Scotland, stands a monument erected to the memory of a dog named Bobby. Bobby's owner died and was buried in the cemetery. However, when Bobby came to the funeral, he refused to leave the grave. As months passed, the local townspeople fed him and often took him into their homes. However, Bobby always went back to his owner's grave. After enduring four years of harsh weather and grief, he finally died – lying on his master's grave – faithful to the end.

I love that powerful old hymn, *"Faith of our Fathers."* Millions of martyrs around our world have suffered and continue to suffer for their faith. The original version of this hymn was first published in 1849. It reads,

> Faith of our fathers, living still
> In spite of dungeon, fire and sword,
> O how our hearts beat high with joy
> Whene'er we hear that glorious word!
> Faith of our father, holy faith
> We will be true to thee till death."[147]

On a modest, small tombstone in Greenmount Cemetery in Baltimore, Maryland, is an inscription with Greek words. The quotation is from Revelation 2:10: "Faithful unto death." The stone marks the resting place of the body of J. Gresham Machen. Machen's "dependability and integrity showed itself in his scholarly devotion to the truth, in his defense of historic Christianity, and in his perseverance in keeping his ordination vows. He was faithful because he believed in a great God."[148]

We've all heard the little prayer, "Now I lay me down to sleep; I pray the Lord my soul to keep; if I should die before I wake, I pray the Lord my soul to take." Prayer is conversation with God. We learn about God through faithful reading of the Bible. When we hear His Word in our hearts, our lives begin to change forever.

It was T. T. Crabtree who said, "Brethren, whatever the good Lord tells me to do in this blessed book, that I'm going to do. If I see in it that I must jump through a stone wall, I'm going to jump at it. Going through it belongs to God, jumping at it belongs to me."[149]

The call to faith is found throughout the New Testament. Catherine W. Marshall writes, "Without faith it is impossible to please God. Nor can we receive anything from God or get anywhere in the Christian life without faith. And in one of the greatest blank-check promises Jesus left us, He pinned everything to faith: 'And whatever you ask in prayer, you will receive, if you have faith.'"[150] I often wonder what people do today without faith.

As a beginning freshman in high school, I remember having just enough money from my summer savings to buy new clothes. As cold weather came, I soon realized the need for a warmer coat. The problem was I didn't have enough money to buy one. So I asked my parents for one. They gave me an old, heavy, gray hand-me-down wool coat. I have no idea how many times it had been passed down through the years. It was very worn and tattered. I hated that old wool coat. It made me itch too.

My mother told me to wear it every day to school. So I put it on each morning until I was out of sight, and then I took it off. After all, I was embarrassed to be seen in it! What would my friends think? Surely everyone would notice me in that old gray coat and make some kind of negative comment.

Later on, as the weather grew colder, I had no choice but to wear it. In fact, it seemed many of my friends were shivering with their new coats on while I was nice and toasty. Just as that old worn and tattered wool coat had faithfully served those before me, it continued to serve me when I needed it most. It kept me warm all winter!

How many professing Christians today just wear their faith on their sleeve? Do they only want to be noticed rather than noticing the presence of God in the lives around them? Do we only want to be fashionable to be faithful Christians? I believe the family of God needs to be faithful, reliable, trustworthy, and loyal.

I wonder what would happen if we asked ourselves what kind of church we would have if everyone was faithful. Would anyone show up for Sunday worship? Would we have enough teachers for our Sunday school classes? Would we be growing as a church numerically and spiritually? I wonder if the church would even exist without the faithful few!

A church choir director was going crazy at the rehearsals for a Christmas choral concert. It seemed at least two or more members of the choir were absent from every rehearsal. Finally, at the last rehearsal, she said, "I want to personally thank the pianist for being the only person in this entire church choir to attend each and every rehearsal during the past two months." Then the pianist stood up, bowed, and said, "It was the least I could do, considering I won't be able to be at the concert tonight." Clearly, the value of even *one* of God's faithful followers is important.

Early one morning, a young jogger went for a run on the beach. An old man walking with a cane was looking to see what the receding tide had exposed. Every once in a while, he bent over to pick something up; then he tossed it back into the ocean.

The jogger watched with interest as he scanned the beach in front of him. Suddenly he realized the old man was looking for starfish! Every time he saw one lying helpless in the sand, he lovingly picked it up and tossed it gently back into the sea. Curious as to why he was doing this, the young jogger asked him about it.

The old man explained, "The starfish are left behind after the tide goes out. If they don't get back into the ocean, they'll dry up and die in the hot sun." The jogger said, "But there are so many miles of beach, and there are millions of starfish. You can't save them all. What difference will it make?" The old man bent over slowly and picked up another starfish. As he tossed it back in the ocean, he looked at the young jogger and said, "It makes a difference to that one."

It's easy to get discouraged and overwhelmed by the sheer magnitude of the mission God has set before us. Sometimes we fail to see the value to Him of each *one*. We're called to be faithful in scanning those beaches in life, making a difference to this *one* and that *one* in Jesus' name. Matthew reminds us, "Therefore go and make disciples in all the nations" (Matthew 28:19 TLB).

We are in constant need of reviving our faith. Revelation tells us to, "Remain faithful even when facing death and I will give you the crown of life" (Revelation 2:10 TLB). Scripture is clear that faithfulness is supposed to be a characteristic of God's people. Jesus warns us, however, that "Salt is good, but if it loses its saltiness, how can you make it salty again? Have salt among yourselves, and be at peace with each other" (Mark 9:50).

Jesus used salt to illustrate three qualities that should be found in all His people. First, we should remember God's faithfulness, just as salt was used with a sacrifice to recall God's covenant with His people (Leviticus 2:13). Second, we should make a difference in the flavor of this world we live in, just as salt changes the flavor of the meat (Matthew 5:13). Third, we should work against moral decay in our society, just as salt preserves food from decay. When we lose this desire to salt the earth with the love and message of God, we become useless to Christ.

Often we hear that it's better to wear out than to rust out. While at a clergy retreat one day, the worship leader spoke about the legend of a wealthy woman who, when she reached heaven, was shown a very plain mansion. She was furious! "Well," she was told, "That is the house prepared for you." "Whose is that fine mansion across the way?" she asked. "It belongs to your gardener," came the reply.

Finally, she asked, "Why does *he* have a house better than *mine*?" She was told, "The houses here are prepared from the materials that are sent up. We don't choose them; you do that by your earthly faithfulness." It's said, "Faith grows as it is used, and weakens and dwindles and possibly dies as it is abused."[151]

If you tell people there are 300 billion stars in the universe, why do they believe you? But if you tell them a bench has just been painted, they have to touch it to be sure. Faith is God's gift to us; it becomes a gift as we accept eternal life.

The gospel, therefore, is a way of faith. The Christian life is a walk of faith. When our faith pleases God, He rewards us. Hebrews says, "And without faith it is impossible to please God, because anyone who comes to Him must believe that He exists and that He rewards those who earnestly seek Him" (Hebrews 11:6).

I believe "Our living faith must become a walking faith."[152] God wants every believer to have the spiritual fruit of faithfulness. First Corinthians tells us, "Now it is required that those who have been given a trust must prove faithful" (1 Corinthians 4:2).

A man with one leg approached Reverend Hudson Taylor, the great missionary who carried the gospel to the interior of China. The man said, "I want to go to China as a missionary." Reverend Taylor asked, "Why do you think you can be a missionary when you have only one leg?" The man replied, "Because I don't see any people with two good legs going."

All Christians should do a self-evaluation. We should ask ourselves, "Do we have two good legs that aren't walking for God?" Maybe now is the time to begin walking for Christ in faithfulness. James 2:26 KJV says, "Faith without works is dead." Often, "When faith in testimony is exercised about things in which we are personally concerned, it will, in proportion to its strength, influence our conduct accordingly."[153]

An old Scotsman once operated a little rowboat business for transporting passengers. One day, a passenger noticed the old man had carved the word *faith* on one oar and the word *works* on the other. Curious, he asked what it meant. The old Christian man was glad to tell him. He said, "I will show you." So he dropped one oar in the water and rowed with the other oar (called *works*), and they just went around in circles. After that, he rowed with one oar again (called *faith*), and the little boat just went around in circles again. However, this time, the boat went in the opposite direction, but it was still going in a circle.

After this demonstration, the old man picked up both *faith* and *works* and began rowing the two oars together. He moved quickly through the water in a straight line. He explained, "You see, that's the way it is in the Christian life. Dead works without faith are useless. Faith without works is dead; we go nowhere (or in circles) by using only one. But when faith and works are pulling together, we move forward with God's blessing. This is called faithfulness in action."

T.T. Crabtree adds, "An authentic faith is one that works. Faith and deeds are not opposites; they are inseparable."[154] As faithful Christians we should "seek to serve God in all His activities, and to transform each task into divine service."[155]

Likewise, "faith produces love. That is Peter's message. Paul's teaching is to the same effect, but from a slightly different point of view. He wrote, "Faith works through love" (Galatians 5:6). Love is the medium through which faith works, it is the atmosphere in which the fruit grow and abound."[156]

As recounted in *Illustrations Unlimited,* by James S. Hewett, Mother Teresa of Calcutta was once asked, "How do you measure the success of your work?" She looked puzzled for a moment and then replied, "I don't remember that the Lord ever spoke of success. He spoke only of faithfulness in love. This is the only success that really counts."[157]

Michelangelo spent countless hours on his back while painting the ceiling of the Sistine Chapel. A friend asked him why he paid so much attention to detail when people would see it only from a distance. "After all," his friend said, "who'll ever notice if it's perfect or not?" Michelangelo responded, "I will."

As Christians, we believe, that "faithfulness flows from faith in God. When our attention is focused on Him, a steadiness and dependability develops as His claims and His law govern our actions."[158]

Faith means following God. It's not found by itself in the New Testament. There will always be verbs after a response of faith. For example, in Hebrews, we see that it was "By faith Abraham … *obeyed,* by faith Jacob … *blessed,* by faith Moses … *refused*" (Hebrews 11:8, 21, 24). Note that, in every instance, a verb follows the word faith.

A hunter once said Sam was his best hunting dog ever. Sam was a dog who found birds and pointed them with excitement. His dog taught him the joy of being in nature. If his point said a bird was hiding in a clump of bushes, it was there. He was more than just a bird dog. Often, they shared lunches in an abandoned apple orchard and fell asleep together.

However, one afternoon, they became separated from one another. Neither was familiar with the area. The hunter called and whistled, but there was no sign of Sam. While heading back to town for an important appointment, he thought, *How could I possibly leave Sam? What if he's lost forever?* Then the hunter remembered a trick an old dog trainer had given him years before. So he unbuttoned his jacket, took off his shirt, and laid it on the ground under a small bush. He worried all night.

Upon returning the next morning, he found Sam, curled up in his shirt with his nose tucked in his sleeve. He looked up and wagged his tail. Sam seemed to say with his large brown eyes, *Where have you been, my friend? I've been waiting for you all night! But I knew you'd come back!*

How often do we get lost in the daily demands of life while trusting God's Word enough to curl up in it? Are we patient enough, knowing that our 'Friend' will come and find us if we keep faith in Him?

Interestingly enough, "A shared faith binds people together in ways that cannot be duplicated by other means."[159] Did you know there are approximately five hundred references to the words *faith* and *belief* in the New Testament?

Accordingly, "Faith is clearly one of the most important concepts in the whole NT. Everywhere it is required and its importance insisted upon. Faith means abandoning all trust in one's own resources. Faith means casting oneself unreservedly on the mercy of God. Faith means laying hold on the promises of God in Christ, relying entirely on the finished work of Christ for salvation, and on the power of the indwelling Holy Spirit of God for daily strength. Faith implies complete reliance on God and full obedience to God."[160]

The first attempt to dig the Panama Canal across the Isthmus of Panama was made by a French company. Men and machinery tackled mountains and jungles. The project was abandoned, however, for a while, not because of the mountains but because of the mosquitoes. Yellow fever killed thousands of workers. American doctors eventually found ways to protect them against the mosquitoes. When the mosquitoes were taken care of, the mountains soon came down.

There's a big difference between the size of mountains and mosquitoes. It's interesting to see how much damage can come from such a small mosquito. More people died from mosquito bites than all the mountainous challenges set before them.

The Bible reminds us that no one succeeds in doing great things when they haven't been faithful in small things. Luke made this clear when he wrote, "Whoever can be trusted with very little can also be trusted with much, and whoever is dishonest with very little will also be dishonest with much" (Luke 16:10).

The word *faithful* is rooted in our basic trust in Christ. We trust our Lord because He is faithful and trustworthy. Second Timothy 2:13 TLB says, "Even when we are too weak to have any faith left, He remains faithful to us and will help us, for He cannot disown us who are part of Himself, and He will always carry out His promises to us." So, "Faith requires faithfulness, for our faith is only as effective as the object or person (God in Christ) in whom it is placed."[161]

A twelve-year-old boy became a Christian during a church retreat. At school the next week, his friends questioned him about the experience. "Did you see God?" asked one friend. "Did you hear

God speak?" another asked. The young boy answered no to all their questions. "Well, how do you know you are a Christian?" they asked. The boy searched for an answer and finally said, "It's like when you catch a fish; you can't see the fish or hear the fish; you just feel it tugging on your line. I just felt God tugging on my heart."

In biblical theology, we see that "faithfulness lies at the heart of the covenant relationship. God pledges consistent fidelity to His promises, and this is why He expresses Himself through covenants. God pledges a lasting relationship, and we are invited – indeed called – to commit our lives with a commensurate *faithfulness*."[162]

CHAPTER 8

GENTLENESS

An airline company was concerned about a high percentage of accidents it was having. So the company decided to eliminate human errors by building a completely automated plane. A voice over the loudspeaker said, "Ladies and gentlemen, it may interest you to know that you are now traveling in the world's first completely automatic plane. Just sit back and relax because nothing can possibly go wrong … go wrong … go wrong … go wrong …"

William Armitage wrote, "Gentleness is the richest ornament of man or woman. The old terms of "gentleman" and "gentlewoman," and "lady," are, to an extent, losing their meaning. Gentle meant at first well born, which carried with it the thought of mildness in character and refinement in manner."[163]

What makes gentleness such a powerful quality? In short, gentleness allows us to grow as Christians. First Thessalonians 2:6–7 tells us, "We were not looking for praise from people, not from you or anyone else, even though as apostles of Christ we could have asserted our authority. Instead, we were like young children among you."

Our society often overlooks gentleness as a positive personal trait. It seems power and assertiveness gain more respect, even though no one likes to be bullied. Gentleness is love in action: being considerate, meeting the needs of others, allowing time for the other person to talk, and being willing to learn. It's an essential characteristic for all God's people to adopt. We should continuously maintain a gentle attitude in our relationships with others.

The eighth quality of the fruit of the Spirit is gentleness (meekness in the KJV). The Greek word, *prautes,* is very difficult to define in English. It is commonly misunderstood. While weakness and frailty are frequently associated with it, there is no such idea in the Greek word. The word *prautes* is probably one of the most difficult to translate.

In the New Testament, we find three meanings. First, it means being submissive to God's will (Matthew 5:5, 11:29, 21:5). Second, it means being teachable and not too proud to learn (James 1:21). Third, and most often of all, it means being considerate (1 Corinthians 4:21; 2 Corinthians 10:1; Ephesians 4:2).

In *Letters to the Galatians,* William Barclay gives Aristotle's definition of *prautes* as the "the quality of the man who is always angry at the right time and never at the wrong time. What throws most light on its meaning is that the adjective *praus*, is used of an animal that has been tamed and brought under control; and so the word speaks of that self-control which Christ alone can give."[164]

Clearly, there's a connection between gentleness and self-control. However, the topic of self-control will be discussed later. All too often, "Old and New Testament gentleness is being replaced by physical, emotional, and environmental abuse. The dynamic balance between power and respect, strength and serving, agape and anger is vanishing. Personal and institutional violence have become the norm."[165]

First Peter 3:15–16 instructs us to "Always be prepared to give an answer to everyone who asks you to give the reason for the hope that you have. But do this with gentleness and respect, keeping a clear conscience, so that those who speak maliciously against your good behavior in Christ may be ashamed of their slander." It should be noted that gentleness is not just "polish and politeness."[166]

As a child, I remember my first family visit to the White Mountains in New Hampshire. We stopped the car at a rest area to eat our picnic lunch. I distinctly remember my father warning me not to lean against an old birch tree standing nearby. Often they are rotten and break easily. As usual, I listened for a brief moment.

My decision to lean against an old birch tree that day proved to be a valuable lesson. No sooner had I leaned against it than it broke! I fell about four or five feet backward into an old culvert below. I remember how wet and rocky it was. In fact, it happened so quickly that I didn't even have a chance to yell!

No sooner had I fallen, however, than I suddenly felt the gentleness of my father's arms carrying me back up the hill. While nothing was broken, I did have a few cuts and bruises to talk about – never mind a bruised ego. While my father had every reason to yell at me and say, "I told you so," he didn't. I learned an important lesson in gentleness that day.

As Christians, we have a biblical command to act with gentleness. This command appears throughout the Bible no less than twenty-three times. Gentleness is always demanded of us in our conduct with God and toward one another. In every scriptural reference to gentleness, we are given a distinct reminder and open invitation to imitate and model our lives after Christ.

Firing an employee must be one of the toughest jobs a supervisor has to face. While humor may be seen in the following story, there is also a message. An insurance sales manager, known for his tact and diplomacy, noticed that one of his young salesmen was performing so poorly he decided to terminate him. The manager called him into his office and said, "Son, I don't know how we're ever going to get along without you, but starting Monday, we're going to try."

In whatever circumstances we find ourselves, it's important to remember that "gentleness is a most necessary part of character building. No life is really noble without it. Nothing compensates for its absence. It may seem a small thing, and yet it is essential."[167]

According to Judith Lechman, in her book, *Spirituality of Gentleness: Growing Toward Christian Wholeness,* we see the essence of gentleness in our attitude toward God and others. She writes, "The Hebrew word used in the Old Testament for gentleness is equally complex and multifaceted. Both speak of power and meekness, oppression and strength, being and doing. The difference between the Greek and the Hebrew is mainly a matter of emphasis. Whereas gentleness in the Old Testament is used primarily to describe our attitude toward God, the New Testament primarily dwells on the manner in which the gentle person treats others."[168]

Oftentimes, a gentle person can help nurture those around them. The apostle Paul described his relationship with the Christians at Thessalonica "as gentle among you as a mother feeding and caring for her own children" (1 Thessalonians 2:7 TLB). We see here a "quiet and peaceful spirit nourishes our souls and encourages growth. Seeds that are sown in this soil will bear fruit."[169] Whenever this spirit of gentleness is part of our lives, we become enriched.

Gentleness also enhances harmonious relationships with others. This indwelling of God's Holy Spirit helps bring peace to those stressful situations in our lives, eliminating worry or fear. Gentleness with strength in humility reflects how we treat others. When we adopt this attribute, we become better stewards of our time and talents for Christ. The anxieties – stress, fears and frustrations – tend to disappear from our lives.

The following story, given to me by a former parishioner, echoes this message. One stormy night many years ago, an elderly couple entered the lobby of a small hotel and asked for a room. The clerk explained that because there were three conventions in town, the hotel was filled. Gently he said, "But I can't send a nice couple like you out in the rain at one o'clock in the morning. Would you be willing to sleep in my room?" The couple hesitated, but the clerk insisted. The next morning, when the man paid his bill, he said, "You're the kind of manager who should be the boss of the best hotel in the United States. Maybe someday, I'll build one for you." The clerk smiled, amused by the older man's little joke.

A few years passed, and the clerk received a letter from the old man. It recalled that stormy night and asked him to come to New York City for a visit. A round-trip ticket was enclosed. When the clerk arrived, his host took him to the corner of Fifth Avenue and 34th Street, where a new magnificent building stood. The older gentleman said, "That is the hotel I built for you to manage." The clerk said, "You must be joking." The old man replied, "I am certainly not." "But who are you?" the hotel clerk asked. "My name is William Waldorf Astor." That hotel was the original Waldorf-Astoria, and the young clerk, George C. Boldt, became its first manager.

Gentleness helps us understand what it's like to walk in someone else's shoes. We should always be mindful that "God initiates gentleness. We respond. Christ calls us to gentleness. We answer. When He commands us to follow Him, to accept His plans for us, to commit ourselves wholeheartedly to Him, and to go the way He goes without questioning, we struggle to echo His gentleness in our attitude and behavior."[170] We should therefore fulfill the psalmist's words, "I delight to do Thy will, O my God: yea, Thy law is within my heart" (Psalm 40:8 KJV).

After church one Sunday, a parishioner handed me a note quoting F.B. Meyer: "I used to think that God's gifts were on shelves one above the other; and that the taller we grew in Christian character the easier we could reach them. I now find that God's gifts are on shelves one beneath the other. It's not a question of growing taller but of stooping lower; that we have to go down, always down, to get His best gifts." Gentleness must always keep growing and developing within us.

To maintain this spirit of gentleness, we need to set goals for accomplishment. In His Sermon on the Mount, Jesus said, "Blessed are the meek, for they shall inherit the earth" (Matthew 5:5 KJV). Sometimes people want their inheritance now and force their points of view on others by demanding certain rights. Jesus points out that this inheritance is for the meek. He will bless us, but we must maintain a spirit of gentleness in the meantime.

The Bible tells us that "the meek shall inherit the earth" (Psalm 37:11 KJV). The words *gentleness* and *meekness* are often translated interchangeably. In Hebrew, both words mean "to be molded." We should remember that in this molding process, "there is plenty of power to make us meek, and we will see it operating within us when we set our sights on the One who is truly meek."[171]

Jesus gave His followers the perfect pattern for holy living. The apostle Paul appealed to his Corinthian converts through the gentleness of Christ. We learn true gentleness in the school of Jesus' teachings and example.

A mother was having a difficult time getting her son to attend school one morning. "Nobody likes me at school," her son said. "The teachers don't, and the kids don't. The superintendent wants to transfer me, the bus drivers hate me, the school board wants me to drop out, and the custodians are against me. I don't want to go!" His mother insisted, "You've got to go! You're healthy. You've a lot to learn. You've got something to offer others. You're a leader. Besides you're forty-nine years old, you're the principal, and you've got to go to school!"

Often, "when God wants a great preacher or a great teacher or a great leader He never goes to the seat of the loafer to get him. God always goes amongst those who are working at the job which is theirs then and there."[172] Christians should be like Christ, who is "strength willingly under control or authority of God and others, expressed in a humble, open, and teachable spirit."[173] I agree that "the church is for 'sweaters' and not for 'sitters.'"[174]

Gentleness makes learning possible, according to the Bible in Second Timothy. It challenges God's people to "not be quarrelsome;

they must be gentle, patient teachers of those who are wrong" (2 Timothy 2:24 TLB). As a teacher, Timothy so often helped those who were confused about the truth. Paul's advice to Timothy was to be humble and patient in teaching God's truth.

Good teaching should never promote quarrelling or foolish arguments. Whether we teach Sunday school, lead a Bible study, or preach in church, we need to listen to the questions from God's people and treat everyone gently and with respect. We must also avoid foolish debates. When we do this, people are more willing to listen to what we have to say and turn from the error of their ways.

Gentleness can help us avoid attitudes that can destroy relationships. Proverbs reminds us that "A gentle answer turns away wrath" (Proverbs 15:1). Gentleness has a way of diffusing an angry person. Why is it that so many people tend to blow things out of proportion and ruin friendships because they aren't gentle enough? "We need gentleness in our marriages, homes, friendships and churches. Gentleness looks with reason at all the facts before passing judgment. The person who shows gentleness acts humanely toward other people. This fruit of the Spirit is vitally needed in our day."[175]

Sometimes gentleness has a way of reminding us of our own shortcomings and failures. In the story about the woman caught in adultery, Jesus teaches us, "Neither do I condemn you … Go now and leave your life of sin" (John 8:11).

While at a dinner party one night, Lady Churchill was seated across the table from her husband, Sir Winston. He kept making his hand walk up and down toward her with two fingers bent at the knuckles. A dinner guest asked, "What is Sir Winston doing while looking at you?" She said, "We had an argument earlier, and he's letting me know it was his fault. He's on his knees making an apology."

Interestingly enough, when a chess game is over, the king and the queen go back in the same box. Someone said that hardening of the heart ages people faster than hardening of the arteries. Just as gentle people build others up, they also strengthen healthier relationships. Gentle actions tend to nourish an attitude of meekness.

Today, however, it seems meekness is as rare as it is unpopular. To many people, meekness seems to carry the idea of being weak or frail. However, this is biblically not true. Meekness is that "inner grace planted by the Spirit. It expresses itself as an unusual strength of character. The truly meek person has a Spirit-given peace which frees him to act gently."[176]

Louis Pasteur once said, "Never try to prove to the other person that you are right. It is human nature to object to anyone who insists he is right. Rather, always present your arguments in such a manner as to do your best to prove that you are wrong. If you follow this approach, especially when you are sure you are right, the person you are trying to convince will bring up strong evidence in behalf of your cause and prove to himself and to the world that your stand is correct."[177]

The shepherd leads gently, but he does lead. The shepherd psalm speaks of passing "through the valley of the shadow of death" (Psalm 23:4 KJV). The Old Testament Hebrews knew there were deep valleys where robbers could hide. It wasn't wise for a shepherd to travel at night or start out so late that he couldn't get his flock safely through such places before dark. Those valleys were dangerous. However, sometimes a shepherd had to lead his flock through some tough places.

Like the disciples, Christian shepherds have similar challenges today. Remember that "gentleness is a quality of controlled power, appropriately applied to constructive purposes and with due regard to the conditions under which the persons concerned find themselves."[178] In addition, "the men and women who in meekness and gentleness and hopefulness assume the burdens of today, and fight the battles of today, and discharge the duties of today, seeing God in whatever honorable and honest task is theirs to perform, can rest assured that if promotion there is, promotion will come!"[179]

"Meekness and gentleness are not the opposites of courage; it takes courage to be meek and gentle in an evil world."[180] A little boy asked a missionary, "Who are the meek?" He responded, "Those who respond with soft answers to tough questions."

Sometimes, however, daily life demands other responses. A case in point involved Booker T. Washington; he traveled to a city to make a speech. As the story goes, his train was late, and he was in a hurry. So he left the station to take a cab, but the driver yelled out, "I don't drive blacks." Washington said, "All right, I'll drive you. You get in the back." Gentleness can often disarm an opponent who wants to fight against someone.

People think because they're smart, strong, rich, or looking out for number one that they'll always be successful. Being assertive seems to be a popular saying today. Although strong people do what they want, they should also be flexible about the needs of others.

The Biblical concept of meekness is much different. In Greek, meekness is commonly used to describe a quality in animals trained by their masters. Even a wild horse can be tamed in time to be gentle and meek. This point helps us understand that our true source of strength and gentleness comes from God.

Humility and meekness are models to follow. They are signs of greatness in anyone's character. Jesus described Himself as "meek and lowly in heart" (Matthew 11:29). Being gentle and considerate of others doesn't mean we have to be weak. Gentleness often comes with strength. It takes inner strength and humility to see our own faults and be willing to improve our lives in Christ. I agree that "it is when we are crucified with Christ, and Christ lives in the soul, that the fruit of meekness will be found. This the Holy Spirit alone can produce."[181]

As we do with all struggles, at first we fail to surrender to God's divine will. We forget Jesus' invitation and command to learn from Him. Jesus said, "Come unto Me, all ye that labour and are heavy laden, and I will give you rest. Take My yoke upon you, and learn from Me; for I am meek and lowly in heart: and ye shall find rest unto your souls. For My yoke is easy, and My burden is light" (Matthew 11:28–30 KJV). When the Spirit produces gentleness within us, others will want the same.

Gentleness "is the spirit of self-restraint in action and leaves no room in the heart for anger, no matter what the provocation. It leaves vengeance to Him to whom it belongs."[182] The Bible says, "Vengeance is mine, I will repay, saith the Lord" (Romans 12:19 KJV). So we see that "meekness is a word meaning to be gentle, kind and not easily provoked. Meekness is humility in action. We could substitute the word humility for meekness, but it must be an active humility, involved in doing something."[183]

Oftentimes, people are too willing to 'toot' their own horns rather than accept a position of humility among others. Eli Perkins said, "A bore is a man that talks so much about himself that you have no chance to talk about yourself."[184] Will Rogers once suggested in a television interview, "Get someone else to blow your horn, and the sound will carry twice as far." Edmond Goncourt adds, "the whole art of pleasing, lies in never speaking of oneself; always, persuading others to speak of themselves. Everyone knows this and everyone forgets it."[185]

Scripture says Moses humbled himself before God. He believed other people could do God's work better. Even though Moses was a poor speaker, God still used him to speak for others. Whether it's singing in the choir, ushering in church, teaching a Bible class, being a missionary, or preaching the gospel, God wants everyone – both great and small – in His service. But are we humble enough to ask the Lord to use us?

It's true that "humble pie is the only pastry that's never tasty."[186] Gentleness has been described as, "an integrity of attitude which strives to see things as they are in the spirit of love. It may be what some academicians refer to as 'objectivity' an attitude of openness which helps us to accept the truth whether we like it or not and even when it runs counter to cherished, previously held concepts."[187]

Do you remember when, in our country's history, only a gentleman's handshake was needed to bind an agreement? Times have certainly changed. We have product maintenance and service agreements, written warrantees and guarantees against defects and malfunctions, pre-nuptial contracts, and vehicle purchase and sales agreements – to list just a few.

Our covenant with one another to be gentle and meek originates in the power of the Holy Spirit. God created all people in His likeness. Gentleness is often a quiet and humble quality. Its presence is often felt without notice. It's like a refreshing, cool breeze on a hot, humid day. This wonderful fruit of the Spirit is so powerful it can build healthy relationships.

I'm sure each of us can probably name one instance in the past week when we failed to maintain our gentle side. How many times have you heard parents reprimand their children for being too rough with each other? Usually the warning is, "Be careful now! The baby isn't as strong as you are. Treat the baby gently!"

So what is true meekness? "It is the spirit of Jesus Christ brought to bear upon human life in all its relations. It is the gentle, loving spirit of the Christian whose mind has been brought into harmony with the mind of Christ, who was meek and lowly of heart."[188]

Colossians 3:12–13 teaches us, "Therefore, as God's chosen people, holy and dearly loved, clothe yourselves with compassion, kindness, humility, gentleness and patience. Bear with each other and forgive one another if any of you has a grievance against someone. Forgive as the Lord forgave you."

According to the book of James, gentleness is also a sign of wisdom. He writes, "But the wisdom that comes from heaven is first of all pure and full of quiet gentleness. Then it is peace-loving and courteous. It allows discussion and is willing to yield to others; it is full of mercy and good deeds. It is wholehearted and straightforward and sincere" (James 3:17 TLB).

Have you ever known anyone who claimed to be wise but acted foolishly? True wisdom is measured by the depth of a person's character. Just as a tree is known by its fruit, we can determine the level of a person's wisdom by the way he or she acts.

How many times have you been tempted to get involved in or encourage conflict, pass on some juicy piece of gossip or fuel the fire with dissention? James asks, "Who is wise and understanding among you? Let them show it by their good life, by deeds done in humility that comes from wisdom" (James 3:13).

Envy and selfish ambition are not attributes that God approves of. It's easy for us to be drawn into making wrong choices as we face society's pressures. Sometimes this even happens to well-meaning Christians. When we hear the words, "Assert yourself! Go for it! Set your goals high," sometimes we're drawn into a downward spiral of self-indulgence and competitive worldliness. When we seek God's wisdom, we are free of comparing our lives to others and the longing to have what they have.

I've heard it said that gentleness blends the harmlessness of a dove with the courage of a lion. There's a story about a lion walking through the jungle, taking a poll to find out which animal was the greatest of them all. When he saw the hippopotamus, he asked, "Who is the king of the jungle?" "You are," said the hippopotamus. Next, he met a giraffe. "Who is king of the jungle?" he asked. "You are," said the giraffe. Then he met a tiger and said, "Who is king of the jungle?" "Oh, you are," said the tiger.

Finally, he met an elephant. The lion gave him a good rap on the knee and said, "And who is king of the jungle?" Immediately the elephant picked him up in his trunk and flung him against a large tree. As the lion bounced off the tree and hit the ground, he got up, dusted himself off, and said, "You don't have to get so mad just because you don't know the right answer!"

We can learn a lot from the lion within us. I wonder how many of the greatest people in the world have been the meekest at some point in their lives. John Bunyan once wrote, "We will come again to this Valley of Humiliation. It is the most fruitful piece of ground in all these parts."[189]

When "Charles Bront was dying he was too proud to call a doctor and even more proud to lie down. He died standing up. Too many Christians are the same way. Others are like the man who prayed, 'Lord, make me a doormat.' When God made that person a doormat and he was trampled upon by others, he complained and manifested an opposite spirit from his prayer."[190]

A newspaper reporter who interviewed an old rancher asked him what attributed to his success. With a twinkle in his eye, the man replied, "It's been about 50 percent weather, 50 percent good luck, and the rest is brains!" At that moment, a young, cocky cowboy rode by and saw the old rancher sitting on his mule. Deciding to have a little fun, the young cowboy drew his six-shooter and told the rancher to get down off his mule. Then he asked him if he had ever danced. The cowboy laughed as he emptied his revolver at the man's feet! Obviously unamused, the old man slowly turned back to his mule and pulled out a shotgun from his pack. He aimed it at the bulletless young cowboy and said, "Did you ever kiss a mule?" The young cowboy said with a trembling voice, "No, but I've always wanted to!"

I suppose there's nothing like a shotgun for motivation. However, the Lord doesn't put a gun to our heads. He does, however, give us stories from the Bible for direction and motivation, but do we listen?

One of the greatest men in history was John the Baptist. He was such a powerful man that many years later, whenever his name was mentioned, people still trembled at the thought of him. According to Matthew, Jesus' eulogy of John reads, "Among those born of women there has not risen anyone greater than John the Baptist" (Matthew 11:11).

When John saw Jesus, instead of giving a speech about his accomplishments, he sent his disciples to Jesus, telling them, "He must increase, but I must decrease" (John 3:30 KJV). When asked who he was, John simply said that he was nobody – just one who is to be heard and not seen. He said he was just, "A voice of one calling in the wilderness" (Matthew 3:3).

Have you ever noticed that David never mentions his victory over Goliath in the book of Psalms? We live in a time when we have the greatest ambassadors, the greatest preachers, the greatest evangelists, and the greatest movie stars. It seems everyone wants a position of dignity and honor, a title to be properly addressed by. It's no wonder that Jesus can't be seen today. Even the apostle Paul said of himself, "I am the least of the apostles" (1 Corinthians 15:9 KJV).

Ben Franklin once said, "The sentence which has most influenced my life is, 'Some persons grumble because God placed thorns among roses. Why not thank God because He placed roses among thorns?' I first read it when but a mere lad. Since that day it has occupied a front room in my life and has given it an optimistic trend."[191]

To be meek means having the ability to see the roses among the thorns rather than complaining about the thorns among the roses. I wonder which one we see. Our answer helps determine whether or not we possess the same gentleness and meekness Jesus so often spoke about. As Christians, when we are gentle in spirit, we fulfill Solomon's image of the lily among thorns. Gentleness comes from within us as we read God's Word.

Paul Tillich, the great twentieth century theologian and philosopher, wrote, "We belong to the Old Creation, and the demand made upon us by Christianity is that we also participate in the New Creation. There is no way that we can share in this change until we let God move through us at will. We cannot turn from 'images of the earthly' to 'images of the heavenly,' to borrow Saint Bernard of Clairvaux's terms, without God practicing His workmanship in us daily."[192] Gentleness should be a characteristic of every Christian. It should not be used whenever we feel like it.

Years ago, I had an egg route with my brothers in Brownville Junction, Maine. It was my job to pull our little red Radio Flyer wagon to make deliveries. An egg truck would provide us with small, medium, large, and extra-large eggs for our customers. Using a degree of gentleness usually meant higher profits, especially when pulling a wagon without shock absorbers! Gentleness should be part of who we are as Christians.

In season and out of season, our lives should be filled with gentleness. James asks, "Who is a wise man and endued with knowledge among you? Let him show out of a good conversation his works with meekness of wisdom" (James 3:13 KJV). Those who desire wisdom should put God's Word into practice in all they do, think, and say. When the Bible speaks about gentleness, it often refers to people willing to allow Jesus to take control of their lives by allowing the Holy Spirit to bring glory to God.

God lends all His creation to us. We are the borrowers, not the owners. "Gentleness in relation to power means deliberate care. A watchmaker could smash a delicate watch with one blow. But this same strength, carefully directed and appropriately applied to various processes of assembly, permits him to construct a mechanical masterpiece."[193]

So how does gentleness provide seasoning to our lives? How will it be expressed as we relate to others through our own unique personalities and styles?

An admirer once asked celebrated orchestra conductor Leonard Bernstein what was the hardest instrument to play. He replied without hesitation, "Second fiddle. I can always get plenty of first violinists, but to find one who plays second violin with as much enthusiasm or second French horn or second flute, now that's a problem. And yet if no one plays second, we have no harmony."[194]

John E. Brown writes,

In these days of testing we often listen for the voice from heaven and listen in vain, and we look for the burning bush, and we look in vain, we expect the vision of the Damascus road, and the vision does not come. God has not forgotten, and the plan for your life has not been changed, but this delay, this silence means that the time is not yet. In His own good time and in His own wonderful way, God will speak when the time for speaking has arrived, and when ready for the work, the work will be placed in your hands. By the meekness and gentleness and hopefulness of Christ, I beseech you. Don't get discouraged![195]

We should keep in mind that meekness is humility in action. Just when we think we've arrived at humility, we risk losing it. This piece of spiritual fruit must be cultivated constantly in our daily lives. When done properly, other people will know it, and God will surely bless us.

Here are some suggestions for cultivating gentleness and humility in our lives:

(1) Spend time daily in the Scriptures. Read them. Study them. Meditate upon them. Memorize a verse a day. (2) Daily submit your life to God's control and influence. Do this the first thing each morning and remind yourself of it several times throughout the day. (3) Pray for others. Become conscious of their needs and burdens. Put your prayers into action by being willing to help bear their burdens. (4) Put others first, your own plans and ambitions second. Avoid the pitfalls of selfishness and self-interests. Listen to others – do not do all the talking. Be genuinely concerned. Pray with them. (5) Consciously test every thought and motive. Bring them into obedience to Christ. Learn to think and act biblically. (6) Be slow in taking offense. Be quick in acknowledging faults in your life that have offended others. Daily examine your life and confess any sin to God. If needed, seek the forgiveness of others. (7) Learn to compliment others. Build them up, do not tear them down. Avoid gossip and negative, destructive criticism. Seek to praise the good points of others. (8) Be willing to accept persecution and trials with joy and longsuffering. Avoid retaliation. Be quick to forgive and overlook the faults of others.[196]

In realizing our own imperfections and unworthiness, gentleness and humility should "work and work and work and work and study and study and study and pray and pray and pray and pray! Keep your eyes on God's mountaintops and God's stars and God's heavens!"[197] As François Fénelon reminds us, "*Gentleness* is Thy work, my God, and it is the work Thou hast given me to do."[198]

CHAPTER 9

SELF-CONTROL

On a cross-country trip many years ago, my family and I traveled through many small western rural communities. According to the locals, cattle ranchers often found their cows wandering off and getting lost. It's a big deal because if you happen to drive into one of these cows, it's considered your fault, and you have to pay the rancher for his cow.

Ask a rancher how a cow gets lost; chances are, he'll reply, "Well, the cow starts nibbling on a clump of green grass, and, when it finishes, it looks ahead to the next clump of green grass. When it finishes there, it looks ahead to the next clump of green grass and starts nibbling on that one. Then it nibbles on yet another clump of grass right next to a hole in the fence. Of course, there's another clump of green grass on the other side the fence, so it nibbles on and on. The next thing you know, the cow has nibbled itself into being *lost*."

This is the way it is with self-control. Sometimes it gets out of control as we wander away from God. Often, "self-control seems to be sufficiently clear. We should exercise control over those areas of ourselves that are not pleasing to God."[199]

We should ask ourselves if this is the whole story about this fruit of the Spirit. The difficulty with a negative approach to the fruit of self-control is that it focuses on problems of the past and our need to control them. We should learn from the past, but self-control involves more than just pulling up weeds. Like all the fruit of the Spirit, we need to understand self-control as pleasing God in all aspects of our lives.

Ebenezer Scrooge had a chance to look at his past, present, and future. In many ways, it was frightening. It's a secular Christmas story with sensitive moments and internal reflection. "I am the ghost of Christmas past," said his partner in nastiness, Jacob Marley. The past made him uncomfortable. The present showed him the faith he saw in his trusted employee's family. He also saw what people thought of him on the streets. While the present helped him reflect on his life, looking at the future ultimately changed him forever.

The Bible also takes a look at the past, present, and future. The apostle Paul suggests this should be the Christian guide for self-control. The key, however, is to see how each of these fruit of the Spirit is linked together in Christian living. The question for us is how to understand self-control in a positive light – with God in control.

According to the *New Bible Dictionary,* self-control "is translated from the Greek word *enkrateia*, which occurs in three New Testament verses. The corresponding adjective *enkrateia* and verb *enkrateuomai* are used both positively and negatively. Another word translated 'temperate', *nephalios*, sometimes carries a restricted reference to drinking, such as is often read into the modern word 'temperance.'"[200]

By the time you finish reading this book, a number of national and world emergencies will probably have occurred, not to mention those in your personal life. Dr. Norman Vincent Peale once said, "The only people who don't have problems are those in the cemeteries." With a twinkle in his eye, he would add, "and some really have problems!" If we have problems, it just means we're still alive! He even joked that if we didn't have any problems, we should get on our knees and ask God to give us some.

Although self-control appears to be last on the list, it's really the greatest of all in many ways. Isaiah 55:8–9 says, "For my thoughts are not your thoughts, neither are your ways my ways," declares the Lord. "As the heavens are higher than the earth, so are my ways higher than your ways, and my thoughts than your thoughts."

Billy Graham wrote, "The history of mankind has largely centered around a battle for the mind. What a person thinks is of utmost importance."[201] Proverbs 16:32 KJV also makes this clear, "He who ruleth his spirit (is better) than he that taketh a city." And finally, Proverbs 23:7 KJV says on the subject, "For as he thinketh in his heart, so is he."

Words or phrases involving our thoughts or the heart occur frequently in the Bible. God wants to control our minds, just as Satan does. Jeremiah 31:33 says, "I will put my law in their minds and write it on their hearts." God said to Joshua, "Keep this Book of the Law always on your lips; meditate on it day and night, so that you may be careful to do everything written in it. Then you will be prosperous and successful." (Joshua 1:8). Isaiah adds, "You will keep in perfect peace those whose minds are steadfast, because they trust in you" (Isaiah 26:3).

Why is it so easy for us to give into temptation and lose self-control? Temptation is part of Satan's cunning plan to separate us from God. The Bible says, "The serpent was the craftiest of all the creatures the Lord God had made. So the serpent came to the woman. "Really?" he asked. *"None* of the fruit in the garden? God says you mustn't eat *any* of it?" (Genesis 3:1 TLB).

Disguised as a cunning serpent, Satan tempted Eve. At one time, Satan was an angel who rebelled against God and was thrown out of heaven. However, Satan does have limitations. Although he tries to tempt everyone away from God, he won't win in the end. In Genesis 3:14–15, God promises that Satan will eventually be destroyed.

Temptation lures us into self-serving lives, which eventually turn us away from God. Temptation is Satan's way of getting us to give up God's way of life. Satan tempted Eve, and she sinned. Since then, he's been busy getting others to do the same. He even tried to tempt Jesus to sin (Matthew 4:1), but Jesus didn't fall for it!

Temptation often feeds off our propensity to be self-sufficient. Satan tempted Eve by getting her to doubt God's goodness. He claimed God was too strict and selfish in not wanting to share with Eve His knowledge of good and evil. Satan made Eve forget all God's gifts and then had her focus on what she couldn't have.

Thomas Moore wrote, "With all the fruits of Eden blest, save only one, rather than leave that one unknown, lost all the rest."[202] Sometimes we fall into trouble when we start dwelling on things we don't have rather than on all God's gifts to us. Whenever we feel sorry for ourselves (by dwelling on what we don't have), we should remember God's gifts and thank Him!

Often, we find that "self-restraint is as necessary as self-expression".[203] We should be careful to think of temperance or self-control in human terms only. According to the Greeks, "the ideal of perfection was based on the achievement by the person of the art of keeping all one's natural drives and instincts under his command through his own efforts. For the Christian, temperance can be understood only in the light of the idea that human perfection is not achieved by self-reliance but by reliance upon God and through the work of Christ and of the Holy Spirit."[204] Actually, self-control should be a matter of common sense.

William Shakespeare wrote, "'Tis one thing to be tempted, another thing to fall."[205] The word *temperance* also means "strength" in Greek. Its English form, however, means "self-control" or "moral courage," which is encouraged by humility. Robert Gage wisely said that he "who rules himself is the greatest of monarchs."[206]

Temptation often comes in subtle forms and seems harmless at first. Deuteronomy 12:30 TLB says, "Don't follow their example in worshipping their gods. Do not ask, 'How do these nations worship their gods?' and then go and worship as they do!" It is clear God didn't want the Israelites to even ask about the pagan religions being practiced around them.

Idolatry permeated the region of Canaan. It was very easy to get caught up in the subtle temptations of seemingly harmless practices. Curiosity can make us fall. Knowledge of evil can be harmful if it's too tempting to resist. It's always best to remain on the side of cautionary discretion and God's Word.

I remember reading a sign on an office door that said, "Lead me not into temptation; I can find it for myself." I'm sure we can all relate to that statement at some point in our lives. Temptation is a daily struggle for many.

There's a story about a man who wanted to give a young bird some worms in exchange for his feathers. So they made a deal: one feather for two worms. The next day, the little bird was flying around with his father. The older bird said, "You know, son, we are the happiest of all the animals. Our wings lift us high in the air, nearer and nearer to God." Unfortunately, the young bird didn't hear his father because all he saw was an old man with worms. Flying down, he plucked two more feathers from his wings and had a feast. This pattern continued day after day. When fall came, it was time to fly south. However, the young bird couldn't fly! He had given up his ability to fly in exchange for worms. This is a constant temptation in our lives – to exchange feathers for worms.

Stephen F. Winward writes, "The body to be controlled is not a tomb; it is a temple of the Holy Spirit. To Plato and the Greeks the body was regarded as the tomb in which the soul was imprisoned."[207] The Bible often describes our difficulty in achieving and maintaining self-control. Temptation hits us hardest when we are most vulnerable and weak.

This was especially true of King Solomon. First Kings 11:1–2 says, "King Solomon, however, loved many foreign women besides Pharaoh's daughter –Moabites, Ammonites, Edomites, Sidonians and Hittites. They were from nations about which the Lord had told the Israelites, 'You must not intermarry with them, because they will surely turn your hearts after their gods.' Nevertheless, Solomon held fast to them in love."

Solomon clearly had some weak points, despite all his wisdom. He couldn't say no to his lustful desires. Whatever his reason for marriage – whether it was to strengthen political ties or to fulfill personal pleasures – he was led into idolatry.

We too can have strong faith, but we can also have our weaknesses. This oftentimes lets temptation get its foot in the door. We have all heard the saying that a chain is only as strong as its weakest link. If Solomon could sin while being the wisest man in the world, then so can we. Hellenic thinking viewed sexual appetites as "bodily appetites governed by the virtue of temperance."[208] However, sometimes God allows His people to go into the fiery furnace while keeping an eye on the clock and a hand on the thermostat.

A clergy friend who liked to golf once told me that golf balls were originally made with smooth surfaces. It was discovered that more distance was gained as the ball got roughed up. So manufacturers decided to make them with dimples. Sometimes the rough journeys we travel help us go further in life.

Billy Graham wrote, "God never tempts any man. That is Satan's business."[209] Temptation can hit our lives anywhere and anytime. Matthew 4:1 says, "Jesus was led by the Spirit into the wilderness to be tempted by the devil." Satan physically tempted Jesus with possessions and power. However, Jesus did not give in.

The Bible says Jesus was, "tempted in every way, just as we are – yet He did not sin" (Hebrews 4:15). Our Lord knows exactly what we're going through. He's ready, willing, and able to help us in all our struggles. In every situation or time of temptation, we can turn to Jesus for strength.

Scientific research has been conducted on certain types of alligators. Being lazy, they rarely hunt for food but usually wait for their victims to cross their paths. Along riverbanks, they appear lifeless, often with their mouths opened wide. It's not long, however, before flies and other bugs gather on the alligators' tongues. Then bigger animals, like frogs and lizards, join the party to eat the insects. Finally, the alligators slam their jaws together, and the party is over!

The lesson here is simple. Don't let yourself fall into temptation, but practice self-control. It helps you "guard against enemies within as well as without, and to be prepared for assaults from all quarters."[210]

I've often wondered why opportunity only knocks once, while temptation bangs at our door all the time. A salesman asked a small boy sitting on the steps of a house, "Is your mother home?" The boy said, "Yes, she's home," and slid to one side to let him pass by. The salesman knocked repeatedly but received no response. So he turned to the little boy and said, "I thought you said your mother was home." The boy replied, "She is; but this isn't where I live!" Remember: temptations are certain to ring your doorbell, but it's your own fault if you invite them in for dinner!

In Scotland, during the early days of aviation, a stunt pilot was selling rides in his single-engine airplane. One day, he got into an argument with an old farmer who asked to take his wife along for a ride at no extra charge. The pilot finally said, "Fine, I'll take you both up for the price of one if you promise me not to say one word during the entire flight. If you make even one sound, the price is doubled." The farmer agreed, and they flew off.

The pilot flew upside down, making twists and turns that would scare most people. However, the farmer didn't make a sound. The pilot finally landed his plane. As the farmer climbed out, the pilot said, "I made moves up there that frightened even me, but you never said a word! You fear nothing!" The old farmer said, "Well, thank you. But I must admit you almost got me when my wife fell out!"

Self-control in Scripture has a larger meaning. It "covers a large sphere of character. It means self-government, self-control, self-restraint. The Christian is to show sobriety of conduct in all the relationships of life."[211]

A man returned to his parked car, only to find substantial damage to the right front section. A note was placed under his windshield wiper. He was happy the person who hit his vehicle left some information. It read, "There are at least twenty people watching me write this. They think I'm putting down my name, address, and phone number. But I'm not!"

Self-control is a way of living and pleasing God by letting His hands rest on the wheel. I'd be happy to let anyone take the wheel in this next story. While vacationing with my family at a lake in New England, I soon learned the meaning of self-control. Coming to shore after a day of fishing in our aluminum boat, I recall grabbing the towline to pull my father ashore. I distinctly remember my dad telling me not to pull the boat in while he was standing up.

However, there was a rock beside the boat that neither he nor I saw at the time. As I was pulling the boat in ever so gently, it hit the rock, and into the lake he went. My dad was in and out of the water so fast that his wallet didn't even get wet! Without hesitation, I dropped the line and ran as fast as I could in the opposite direction!

Depending on who is recounting this story, however, a slightly different version might be told. Actually, my father was pretty good about it. He didn't get angry. In fact, he even laughed when it happened.

In his book, *Parents and Teenagers*, Jay Kesler points out that "Anger is not always wrong. Loss of temper is wrong."[212] The Bible reminds us that our anger must be held in check and in control. James says, "…human anger does not produce the righteousness that God desires" (James 1:20).

Have you ever noticed how some teens never listen until their parents get angry with them? Then they quickly realize the importance of the situation. Sometimes, however, it's better to blow off a little steam rather than letting the situation get any worse.

If resolution isn't readily found, unresolved issues tend to bring resentful silence instead of loving patience. Of course, as parents, we need to apologize if our words or actions are unreasonable or uncalled for. Usually our children will forgive us and hold no grudges if the apology is sincere. These are good lessons and examples for our children to follow as well. Oftentimes, they will learn how to deal with life situations by watching how we act or react.

"The appetites must be controlled and calmed," Cicero wrote to his son. "We must take infinite pains not to do anything from mere impulse or at random without due consideration and care. For nature has not brought us into the world to act as if we were created for play or jest but rather for earnestness and for some more serious and important pursuits."[213]

Speaking of controlling appetites, a pastor went to see an elderly widow in his church. While visiting her, he noticed a bowl of peanuts on the coffee table. He ate all of them. When the pastor apologized, she said, "It's okay. Don't worry about it because I had all my teeth pulled out three weeks ago. Ever since then, I've just been sucking the chocolate off those peanuts and putting them in that bowl." I'm sure that would cure anyone's appetite; it's a valuable lesson in self-control!

Self-control is seen as a "self-command, or the governing of one's self. The earlier ethical writers among the Greeks, those of the school of Socrates, first determined its meaning to be a proper moderation of our passions and appetites, but especially those for food and drink."[214]

It's said that strength is the ability to break a chocolate bar into pieces with your bare hands and then eat just one piece. Self-control is broadly defined. It includes restraint in every likely scenario; and in the "mastery of every appetite, temper and passion."[215]

A family invited their pastor and his wife for dinner on a very hot Sunday. As they were all seated, the father turned to his six-year-old son and asked him to say grace. However, his son complained, "But, Daddy, I don't know what to say!" So his mother spoke up and said to him, "Just say what you've heard me say." He bowed his little head obediently and said, "O Lord, why did I invite these people here on a hot day like this?"

So what areas of your life control you? Is it food, money, other people's time, substance abuse, or something else? I suspect most of us lack self-control in some area. For me, it's my love for most sweets; especially Hershey's M&M chocolate covered peanuts! (And I always make sure the chocolate coating is on!)

We're indeed a generation concerned with self-control. I've been told by the year 2020, we will have 100,000 people over one hundred years old! While many more people will be living longer, it's believed they will also be healthier. The next generation of elderly people will be the joggers, swimmers, dieters, and low-cholesterol people. Like me, they like to eat yogurt and salads for lunch. Someone once said that people lose weight not by talking about it, but by keeping their mouths shut.

A young recruit turned his nose up at the Army stew and complained to the mess sergeant, "Don't I have any choice here?" The sergeant said, "You certainly do, soldier. Take it or leave it!" Self-control is seen as "discipline towards moderation in matter of bodily or physical pleasure, attainment, or abuse, as well as interpersonal relationships."[216]

An advertisement for a handkerchief factory once said, "Let us stick your nose in our business." An old story about three pastors who went fishing together in northern Canada make this point clear. As they began to get to know each other better, they shared their innermost thoughts. One confessed certain sins he was guilty of. He named them and then asked the other two to confess their weaknesses. The second pastor confessed his sins in detail. The third pastor, however, remained silent for quite a while. Finally, when asked to reveal his weaknesses, he said, "Friends, I don't think you want to know my weaknesses, but since you've asked, I am going to tell you. I just *love* to gossip; and I can't *wait* to get home!"

A Sunday bulletin once listed the pastor's sermon title as "Gossip." Immediately following his message, however, the music director invited everyone to sing, "*I Love to Tell the Story!*" I remember a woman in church once said to me, "I can keep a secret, but the people I tell it to can't." Ben Franklin adds, "A slip of the foot you may soon recover, but a slip of the tongue you may never get over."[217] There is truth in the old saying that a spoon always seems twice as large when you have to take a dose of your own medicine.

Jesus said, "For the mouth speaks what the heart is full of. A good man brings good things out of the good stored up in him, and an evil man brings evil things out of the evil stored up in him. But I tell you that everyone will have to give account on the Day of Judgment for every empty word they have spoken. For by your words you will be acquitted, and by your words you will be condemned" (Matthew 12:34–37).

It's been estimated that most people speak enough in one week to fill a large five-hundred-page book. In the average lifetime, this would amount to three thousand volumes or 1.5 million pages! It's frightening to think that by our words we shall either be acquitted or condemned. Consider this: The Lord's Prayer contains 68 words; the Gettysburg Address has 269; the Ten Commandments has 288; the Declaration of

Independence has 1,342; and in one U.S. government order setting the price of cabbage, there are 26,911 words.

It's not how long we talk but what we say that's so important. James 3:5–6 says, "Likewise, the tongue is small part of the body, but it makes great boasts. Consider what a great forest is set on fire by a small spark. The tongue also is a fire, a world of evil among the parts of the body. It corrupts the whole body, sets the whole course of one's life on fire, and is itself set on fire by hell."

James 3:7–10 continues, "All kinds of animals, birds, reptiles and sea creatures are being tamed and have been tamed by mankind, but no human being can tame the tongue. It is a restless evil, full of deadly poison. With the tongue we praise our Lord and Father, and with it we curse human beings, who have been made in God's likeness. Out of the same mouth come praise and cursing. My brothers and sisters, this should not be."

Veteran actor Ernest Borgnine once said he shied away from certain job offers because he refused to appear in movies that he called "puke." He said he turned down more pictures than you could shake a stick at simply because he refused to swear in motion pictures.

This reminds me of an old woman who was shocked by the language used by two men repairing telephone wires near her home. She even wrote a letter to the company complaining about it. The foreman was asked to report immediately to his supervisor. He said, "Well, you see, me and Joe Wilson were on this job. I was up on the telephone pole when hot lead accidently fell on Joe's neck. So he calmly spoke up to me, 'You really should be more careful, Harry.'"

Often, "for every great temptation there will be many small ones. Wolves and bears are more dangerous than flies, but we are bothered most by flies."[218] Sometimes we don't realize the influence we have on those around us. While shopping, a clerk handed a little boy a lollipop. His mother said, "What do you say?" He replied, "Charge it!"

A major source of argument in the home today is worry about money. This has certainly been the case in my years of pastoral counseling experience. I suppose there are two ways to solve this dilemma: earn more money or simply live within your means! In any event, either plan should work just fine. After awhile, people will worry less and may actually save some money.

Real commitment requires self-control. It's "simple, total acceptance of the idea that everything that God made is sacred and permanently significant. It is the attitude of stewardship. The world is God's. We are users and possessors of that which we did not invent and of resources which we did not produce."[219]

So how do we resist temptation and still maintain self-control? The ability to resist temptation is based on becoming aware of it when it faces us. The Garden of Eden story is clear. Genesis 3:6 says, "When the woman saw that the fruit of the tree was good for food and pleasing to the eye, and also desirable for gaining wisdom, she took some and ate it."

So why didn't Eve resist temptation? First, we should realize that not all temptation is sin. Giving in to temptation is what leads to sin. Prayer is the antidote to temptation. It helps to say *no* when we know something is wrong. The Lord's Prayer says, "And lead us not into temptation, but deliver us from evil" (Matthew 6:13 KJV).

The Bible says we will have blessings and rewards when we don't give in to our temptations. "Blessed is the one who perseveres under trial because, having stood the test, that person will receive the crown of life that the Lord has promised to those who love Him" (James 1:12). We should be vigilant as we watch for those red warning signs of temptation all around us. The apostle Paul adds, "Do you not know that in a race all the runners run, but only one gets the prize? Run in such a way as to get the prize" (1 Corinthians 9:24).

Many runners crowd together at the starting line of the marathon race. When the pistol is fired, they begin the race. Twenty-six miles later, they're headed toward the finish line, but only one person will get the prize. Paul seems to have been impressed by the stamina, skill, and temperance of athletes. Self-control involves a goal to follow a set list of training rules and regulations with unrelenting effort.

Paul is saying runners should physically put everything into running that race. They shouldn't be thinking about their next meal or about getting blisters on their feet. Their objective is to use all their physical strength to complete the race. Reaching the finish line proves a runner is successful.

We too should run the race to win the prize. However, it's a spiritual race we find ourselves in. Often, "to win, our bodies must be controlled by our souls. Self-control means mastery."[220] When we do this fruit of the Spirit well, we do our best for God.

We shouldn't settle for second place. We should always apply our best efforts, abilities, and talents. God gives us the capability and ability to improve. Otherwise, pain and suffering will overwhelm and even defeat us. If we keep our eyes on the goal ahead, we will have victory in Christ Jesus; He provides us with strength and endurance.

I've heard it said that few speed records are broken when people run from temptation. This reminds me of my high school track and field days. One thing I never forgot was my coach's words, "When you run, don't run to the finish line, but run *through* it!"

I still remember that old television ad encouraging us to eat our Wheaties every morning, "the breakfast of champions." We must have a "constant, sustained effort. I am running … I am fighting … I am buffeting …"[221] Notice that all the verbs used are in the present tense. We know this process is frustrating for many Christians. Remember: frustration is like buying a new boomerang and finding it impossible to throw the old one away!

Shortly after opening his first plant, Thomas Edison noticed his employees were in the habit of watching the factory's only clock. As a hard-working inventor, he didn't show his disproval openly but simply placed dozens of clocks around the factory, with no two showing the same time. After that, there was so much confusion the workers stopped watching the clocks.

Interestingly enough, most people want to leave their temptations behind but still want to keep in contact with them. We're all familiar with those electronic tags attached to clothing, shoes, and other items to prevent theft. If the device is tampered with, removed, or someone tries to walk out of the store with merchandise, an alarm sounds, and another thief is caught.

Sin also rings an alarm in God's ears. He sees and knows everything we do in thought, word, and deed. The only way to avoid being caught is to resist temptation. For those who feel they've gotten away free, they would do well to remember God's final judgment.

Scripture teaches us to resist temptation right away because the longer we wait the worse it is. Second Samuel 11:2 TLB says, "One night he (David) couldn't get to sleep and went for a stroll on the roof of the palace. As he looked out over the city, he noticed a woman of unusual beauty taking her evening bath." As the story goes, after seeing her beauty, David was filled with lust. Perhaps he should have left the area completely to avoid temptation. Instead, he inquired about Bathsheba, and the result was devastating.

Nancy Reagan's advice against drug abuse was to "Just Say No." Richard Walters adds, "Part of renewing the mind is to push unhealthy thoughts away by bringing in good thoughts. Nothing is better than the Word of God!"[222]

The Psalmist says, "Blessed is the one who does not walk in step with the wicked or stand in the way that sinners take or sit in the company of mockers, but whose delight is in the law of the Lord, and on who meditates on His law day and night" (Psalm 1:1–2). Proverbs 16:3 KJV reminds us to "Commit thy works unto the Lord, and thy thoughts shall be established."

We often find, "preparation, or preventive maintenance is one key component of self-control."[223] Furthermore, "there is no area of life excluded from the will of God for the temperate Christian. He is admonished to be temperate 'in all things.' This means that he is to discover and apply the will of God to the whole scheme and scope of life."[224] This is why every Christian needs a plan of action when it comes to temptation and self-control.

Someone once made the analogy that people are like potatoes. From my potato-picking days in Aroostook County, Maine, I know potatoes have to be spread out and sorted (after being harvested) to get the maximum market price. They're often divided according to size: large, medium, and small. It's only after potatoes have been sorted and bagged that they are loaded on to trucks.

However, one potato farmer never bothered to sort his potatoes at all! Yet he seemed to be making the most money. A puzzled neighbor finally asked him, "What is your secret?" He said, "It's simple. I just load up the wagon with potatoes and take the roughest road to town. During the eight-mile trip, the little potatoes always fall to the bottom. The medium potatoes land in the middle, while the big potatoes rise to the top!" That is true not only for potatoes; it can be a law for life. As big potatoes rise to the top on rough roads, tough people can rise to the top in rough times.

Just as this farmer had a plan to sort potatoes by size, Christians also need a plan to sort through life's temptations by using self-control. Developing a plan of self-control should include the "entire consecration of the heart to the glory of God. The heart is the fountain, and all the issues from it must be like itself. The pure in heart have a more than 'Midas-touch', transmuting the occasions of temptation into aids of holiness. With the helmet of hope, the shield of faith, the breastplate of righteousness, and greaves of the preparation of the gospel of peace, the Christian is unconquerable."[225]

In addition, "we exercise control over ourselves when we have some clear ambition or aim."[226] A plan to resist temptation involves asking God through prayer to help us stay away from tempting people, places, and situations. Memorizing and meditating on God's Word helps us combat our weaknesses. Ultimately, it is God who can fill our true needs, but we must trust Him. It's always helpful to share our struggles with another Christian believer when temptation strikes.

We should allow the Holy Spirit to guide our thoughts and actions. Martin Luther once wrote, "God delights in our temptations and yet hates them. He delights in them when they drive us to prayer; He hates them when they drive us to despair."[227]

While temptation may seem harmless, it carries harmful consequences. Plato once contrasted the roles of the cook and the physician in relation to the body. He wrote, "The cook ignorantly ministers to what the body wants; the doctor ministers to what he knows the body needs, that is, to its health."[228]

Matthew 4:2–3 says, "After fasting forty days and forty nights, He was hungry. The tempter came to Him and said, "If you are the Son of God, tell these stones to become bread." As noted earlier, the devil – also called the tempter – tempted Eve in the Garden of Eden. Now he's tempting Jesus in the desert. Satan is a fallen angel. We need to know he is real and fights continually against God's people. Satan is always trying to get us to live his way rather than God's way. When temptation seems overwhelming in your life or when you rationalize giving in, just remember: Satan may be trying to block God's purposes for your life.

Often medicine bottles warn users to shake contents *well* before using. Sometimes God has to do this with us! He has to shake us *well* before we can be of any use to Him. Our service to God often includes times of testing. Remember: God's plan and purpose at every temptation crossing is to make us more valuable.

Years ago a five-dollar bar of steel cut into ordinary horseshoes was worth ten dollars. A five-dollar bar of steel cut into needles was worth $350.00. The same bar of steel cut into delicate springs for watches was worth $250,000.00. So the next time you get discouraged about what God is putting you through, think of that bar of steel!

When the Holy Spirit lives in us, we develop more trust in God. More confidence brings more comfort in times of trial and suffering. God will help us when we feel our lives are out of control. It's like having a guardrail for protection on this road we call life. Jesus said, "Whoever wants to be my disciple must deny themselves and take up their cross and follow me" (Matthew 16:24). Remember that "each temptation leaves us better or worse; neutrality is impossible."[229]

Temptation in of itself is not sin. Even Jesus was tempted by the devil, and He never sinned! However, we sin when we give in to temptation and disobey God. We should never be surprised when temptation appears in those unlikely times and places of our lives. Jesus wasn't tempted inside the temple or during His baptism. He was tempted in the desert where He was hot, tired, hungry, alone, and, most of all, vulnerable.

Satan often tempts us when we're most vulnerable – during times of physical or emotional stress. We're also tempted during times of loneliness and fatigue, when making big decisions or being faced with uncertainties about the future. Satan can also tempt us when we feel we are on top of the world or in a prideful state. We must remain on guard against temptation in any situation, no matter what direction it comes from. William Barclay wrote, "Temptation is not meant to make us fail; it is meant to confront us with a situation out of which we emerge stronger than we were."[230]

Metal is often tested far beyond any necessary stress level. This is done before it can be put to any useful purpose. We, like Jesus, are often tested by God before He can use us for His purposes. Temptation isn't meant to lure us into sin; it enables us to conquer sin. It's not meant to make us bad or weak but to make us good and stronger as Christians. As difficult as life's struggles sometimes are, we can have "hope in conflict, hope of victory, and hope of reward."[231]

The father of a small boy would occasionally sneak into a neighbor's orchard and pick some of the best fruit. He always made sure, however, that the coast was clear. One day, he took his son with him to the orchard. After looking carefully in every direction and seeing no one, he crawled under the fence. Just as he was about to help his son across, the little boy yelled out, "Dad! Dad! You didn't look *up!* You forgot to see if God is watching." When temptation comes our way and we think no one else is watching, remember that God is!

Mastering temptation means letting God master us first. We'll never win over temptation if we pretend it doesn't exist in the first place. We can't make the mistake of thinking it won't happen to us. In everything we should thank God for giving us victory over temptation. We change only with God's help. Change never comes quickly or easily and is never automatic.

Scripture says, "It took seven years of war to accomplish all of this" (Joshua 11:18 TLB). When we read the Bible text, we find the conquest of Canaan seems to have happened quickly, but it actually took seven years. We often expect a quick fix or change in our lives to gain victory over sin. However, our journey with God is a lifelong process.

Changes and victories often take time. Sometimes it's easy for us to lose patience with ourselves and with God when things move too slowly. The things directly in front of our eyes are often hard to see. When we're too close to a situation, it's difficult to see any progress. But God never abandons us.

God has the ability to change even the worst things in our lives. The gospel of John says, "Many of the Samaritans from that town believed in Him because of the woman's testimony, 'He told me everything I ever did'" (John 4:39). The woman immediately began sharing her experience with others. In spite of her reputation, many people accepted her invitation to meet Jesus. Even though we may feel our past sins are too shameful, Jesus has a way of changing us from the inside out.

So how can we change when we're caught up in the devil's trap? Again, Scripture says God wants to change us on the inside. We should, "be assured, that to maintain 'temperance,' we need to remember the Christian life is a conflict, that the victory will always be disputed, that we carry the combatants within, and that the battle-ground is our own heart."[232]

Years ago, I learned that ganglia nerves are the tiniest nerves. They cover our bodies in such a way that even a simple pin prick can send us pain and give warnings. This warning system helps protects our bodies. Like ganglia nerves, we must have the same sensitivity that warns us when dangers approach our spiritual lives.

There's an old adage that says as long as the ship is in the water, everything is all right. When the water gets in the ship, there is big trouble. Matthew 15:19 TLB says, "From the heart come evil thoughts, murder, adultery, fornication, theft, lying and slander."

Oftentimes, we work hard to keep our outward appearance attractive, but what's in our hearts is more important. The way we are deep down – where others can't see – matters greatly to God. As Christians, God makes us different on the inside. This process of Christian change happens when we invite God into our lives. We should eat healthy meals and exercise, and seek to have healthy motives and thoughts.

Our bodies are to be temples where the Holy Spirit lives. What *house-keeping* needs to be done in your home before God lives in it? It's suggested that "our hearts, our members, our eyes, our ears, our tongues, should all be kept holy, because they are set apart to the Lord."[233] Pythagoras wrote, "No man is free who cannot command himself."[234] Sometimes this means being personally accountable for our actions and having the ability to hear that inner voice of God.

God's changes are made complete in us. Scripture makes this clear in 2 Corinthians 5:17, "Therefore, if anyone is in Christ, the new creation has come: The old has gone, the new is here!" As Christians, we are to be brand new on the inside. When the Holy Spirit gives us new life, we are meant to change. We're not just renewed or rehabilitated but *recreated* in union with Christ (Colossians 2:6–7). This new transformation means new life in Christ.

According to William Barclay, "It was Paul's belief and experience that the Christian died with Christ and rose again to a life, new and clean, in which the evil things of the old self were gone and the lovely things of the Spirit had come to fruition."[235] With inward changes, outward changes will come. Here is John the Baptist's advice: "...prove that you have turned from sin by doing worthy deeds" (Matthew 3:8 TLB).

John also called on people to change their behavior. God is watching to see if our outward changes match what's on the inside. God often judges our words by our actions. Just as a good tree produces good fruit, so too should God's people produce good fruit.

Christians are not useful to God if they simply do nothing with their gifts and talents. As in Jesus' day, we can't be Christians in name only. If others can't see our faith and love in Christ, then how will they see God through us? The apostle Paul says, "I am crucified with Christ: nevertheless I live; yet not I, but Christ liveth in me" (Galatians 2:20 KJV).

Additionally, "because Christ lives in him, life is under control. It is God's control rather than Paul's self-interest. It results in Paul's total life commitment to seeking the well-being of those whom God loves. Such a one is temperate: possessed of a self-control which is the operation of the Holy Spirit in love."[236]

Self control calls for total commitment. People have died trying to save others from drowning or rescue them from burning buildings. There's no in between; it's all or nothing. Sometimes extreme measures are needed in extreme circumstances. Self-control is like that. There's no less commitment needed in situations demanding daily sacrifice.

Speaking of total commitment, there's an old story about a chicken and a pig who wanted to open a new restaurant. The chicken said to the pig, "I can provide the eggs, and you can provide the bacon." The pig said, "For you, that would only be a partial commitment, but for me, it's a total commitment!" Self-control requires total commitment.

Change also needs to include repentance. In the gospel story of the woman caught in adultery, we read that "Jesus straightened up and asked her, "Woman, where are they? Has no on condemned you?" "No one, sir," she said. "Then neither do I condemn you," Jesus declared. "Go now and leave your life of sin" (John 8:10–11).

When Jesus challenged those who had not sinned to cast the first stone, all the religious leaders began to quietly leave. Jesus didn't condemn the woman accused of adultery, but neither did He ignore or condone her sin. He simply told her to leave her life of sin. Jesus is always ready, willing, and able to forgive us our sins, but confession and repentance must go hand in hand with changing hearts and minds. With God's help, we can accept God's forgiveness for our sins as we change our behavior.

This transformation, however, requires self-discipline. But how does God help us with that? It's said that "discipline or self-control is freedom within limitations in relationships and our physical well being. By understanding God's principles and teachings we know

His limitations on such things as the use of the tongue, fornication, adultery and gluttony. We are to avoid situations in which we are tempted to commit what is explicitly forbidden in Scripture."[237]

We know there's a wrong way to do right things, but there's never a right way to do wrong things. Unless we're able, through prayer, to keep the lines of communication open with God, we'll eventually give in to the ways of the world. Remember: "When an ostrich buries its head in the ground to avoid unpleasant facts, it only represents an undignified spectacle; it also constitutes an irresistible target."[238]

Our response to discipline often determines how much we benefit from it. Lao Tzu wrote, "He is strong who conquers others; he who conquers himself is mighty."[239] The apostle Paul adds, "Do not conform to the pattern of this world, but be transformed by the renewing of your mind. Then you will be able to test and approve what God's will is – His good, pleasing and perfect will" (Romans 12:2).

As with all spiritual fruit, self-control helps provide choices for us to move in the direction of empowerment. I love the words of that wonderful hymn, *"Have Thine Own Way Lord,"* written by Adelaide A. Pollard. It reads,

> Have Thine own way, Lord!
> Have Thine own way!
> Thou art the potter; I am the clay.
> Mold me and make me after Thy will,
> While I am waiting, yielding and still.
> Hold o'er my being absolute sway.
> Fill with thy Spirit till all shall see
> Christ only, always, living in me![240]

When we team up with God in our spiritual journeys and do His will, self-control becomes a natural response. We should never overestimate the importance of self-control in our daily lives. Remember: we can't beat these temptations alone. We continually need God's help and guidance to succeed. We have every reason to develop this fruit of the Spirit. Self-control sets us free from the sins that weigh us down; it also gives assurance of forgiveness from the Holy Spirit when we do sin.

I shall close with the following words from the apostle Paul's letter to the Philippians. He writes, "Finally, brothers and sisters, whatever is true, whatever is noble, whatever is right, whatever is pure, whatever is lovely, whatever is admirable – if anything is excellent or praiseworthy – think about such things. Whatever you have learned or received or heard from me, or seen in me – put it into practice. And the God of peace will be with you" (Philippians 4:8–9).

ENDNOTES

[1] Billy Graham, *The Billy Graham Christian Worker's Handbook* (Minneapolis: World Wide Publications, 1996), 158.

[2] William J. Armitage, *The Fruit of the Spirit* (London: Marshall, 1907), 8.

[3] Arnold Prater, *The Presence: The Ministry of the Holy Spirit* (Nashville: T. Nelson, 1993), 141.

[4] William Barclay, *The Letters to the Galatians* (Philadelphia: Westminster Press, 1976), 49-50.

[5] Graham,195.

[6] Harry J. Wilmot-Buxton, *The Tree of Life: Plain Sermons on the Fruit of the Spirit* (London: Skeffington Press, 1898), 5-6.

[7] J.D. Douglas, *New Bible Dictionary* (Wheaton: Tyndale House Publishers, 1986), 710.

[8] John H. Timmerman, *The Way of Christian Living* (Grand Rapids: W.B. Eerdmans, 1987), 30.

[9] Karl A. Olsson, *Seven Sins and Seven Virtues* (New York: Harper, 1962), 121.

[10] Jay Kesler, *Family Forum* (Wheaton: Victor Books, 1984), 444.

[11] Graham, 193.

[12] Douglas, 710.

[13] Richard F. Houts, *Fruit of the Spirit* (Pasadena: Fuller Evangelistic Association, 1988), 7.

[14] T.T. Crabtree, *The Zondervan 1986 Pastor's Annual* (Grand Rapids: Zondervan Publishing House, 1985), 15.

[15] Wilmot-Buxton, 18.

[16] John W. Sanderson, *The Fruit of the Spirit: A Study Guide* (Grand Rapids: Zondervan Publishing House, 1976), 61.

[17] Catherine Wood Marshall, *The Helper* (Waco: Word Books, 1978), 172.

[18] Timmerman, 47.

[19] Armitage, 20.

[20] Houts, 16.

[21] William Barclay, 50.

[22] Armitage, 23.

[23] Stephen F. Bayne, *Enter with Joy* (Greenwich: Seabury Press, 1961), 73.

[24] Timmerman, 49.

[25] George W. Bethune, *The Fruit of the Spirit* (Swengel: Reiner Publications, 1976), 52.

[26] John William Reeve, *Lectures on some of the Offices and the Fruit of the Holy Spirit* (London: J. Nisbet, 1863), 194.

[27] James S. Hewett, *Illustrations Unlimited* (Wheaton: Tyndale House Publishers, Inc., 1988), 278–279.

[28] Ibid., 92.

[29] Robert Gage. *Cultivating Spiritual Fruit* (Schaumburg, IL: Regular Baptist Press, 1986}.

[30] Houts, 16.

[31] Hewett, 404.

[32] Sanderson, 75.

[33] Paul Lee Tan, *Encyclopedia of 7000 Illustrations* (Rockville: Assurance Publishers, 1979), 990.

[34] Bob Phillips, *Phillips' Book of Great Thoughts & Funny Sayings* (Wheaton: Tyndale House Publishers, Inc. 1993), 240.

[35] Edythe Draper, *Draper's Book of Quotations for the Christian World* (Wheaton: Tyndale House Publishers, Inc., 1992), 8451.

[36] Tan, 988.

[37] Ibid, 991.

[38] Wilmot-Buxton, 61.

[39] Larry Richards and Norm Wakefield, *Fruit of the Spirit* (Grand Rapids: Zondervan, 1981), 43.

[40] Sanderson, 79.

[41] Ibid, 79.

[42] Armitage, 29.

[43] Wilmot-Buxton, 52.

[44] Timmerman, 87.

[45] Robert Fulghum, *All I Really Need to Know I Learned in Kindergarten* (New York: Ivy Books, 1988), 5–6.

[46] Houts, 16.

[47] Barclay, 16.

[48] Armitage, 39.

[49] E. Draper, 8388.

[50] Houts, 10.

[51] Reeve, 22.

[52] Richards and Wakefield, 68.

[53] Graham, 223.

54 Jay Kesler, *Parents and Teenagers* (Wheaton: Victor Books, 1984), 50.

55 Gage, 81.

56 Bethune, 89.

57 Ibid, 91.

58 Crabtree, 187.

59 Phillips, 83.

60 Timmerman, 95–96.

61 Wilmot-Buxton, 81.

62 Tan, 985.

63 Reeve, 249.

64 Maurice L. Draper, *The Gifts and Fruit of the Spirit* (Independence: Herald Publishing House, 1969), 146.

65 Thomas Oden, *Pastoral Theology-Essentials of Ministry* (New York: Harper and Row Publishers, 1983), 257.

66 Sanderson, 87.

67 Wilmot-Buxton, 86.

68 E. Draper, 8398.

69 Tan, 996.

70 Houts, 10.

71 Wilmot-Buxton, 82.

72 Timmerman, 88.

73 Dennis Waitley, *Seeds of Greatness* (Old Tappan: Fleming H. Revell, 1983), 200.

74 Hewett, 160.

75 Graham, 221.

76 Crabtree, 186.

77 Graham, 221.

78 Houts, 12.

79 Ibid, 16.

80 Richards and Wakefield, 74.

81 Tan, 704.

82 Timmerman, 106.

83 Stephen F. Winward, *Fruit of the Spirit* (Grand Rapids: W.B. Eerdmans, 1984), 135.

84 Sanderson, 102–103.

85 Tan, 701.

86 Richards and Wakefield, 79.

87 E. Draper, 6644.

88 Timmerman, 105.

89 Hewett, 117.

90 Timmerman, 105.

91 Richards and Wakefield, 78.

92 Hewett, 293–294.

93 Tan, 707.

94 Timmerman, 102.

95 Hewett, 287.

96 Bethune, 131.

97 Oden, 305.

98 Billy R. Hearn, *Communion – A Songbook for God: People in Harmony* (Canoga Park: Birdwing, 1978), 43.

99 Houts, 16.

100 Douglas, 434.

101 Gage, 95.

102 Millard Erickson, *Christian Theology* (Grand Rapids: Baker Book House, 1986), 375.

103 Walter A. Elwell, *Evangelical Dictionary of Theology* (Grand Rapids: Baker Book House 1985), 470.

104 Fulghum, 78.

105 Douglas, 433.

106 E. Draper, 5063.

107 Richards and Wakefield, 88.

108 Sanderson, 114.

109 Armitage, 55.

110 Sanderson, 112.

111 Tan, 1525.

112 Timmerman, 110.

113 Hewett, 195.

114 Ibid.

115 M. Draper, 4644.

116 Bayne, 130.

117 Winward, 156.

118 Wilmot-Buxton, 73.

119 Timmerman, 110.

120 Hewett, 56.

121 James C. Galvin, *Life Application Bible* (Iowa Falls: Tyndale House Publishers, 1990), 334.

122   Ibid., 111.
123   Carlton R. Young, *The United Methodist Hymnal* (Nashville: Abingdon Press, 1990), 591.
124   Reeve, 264.
125   Armitage, 55.
126   Sanderson, 114.
127   Timmerman, 108.
128   Tan, 707.
129   Galvin, 1981.
130   Graham, 305.
131   Bethune, 127.
132   Douglas, 433.
133   Young, 224.
134   Ibid, 140–141.
135   Kesler, 230.
136   E. Draper, 3797.
137   Gage, 108.
138   Tan, 404.
139   Olsson, 104.
140   Douglas, 366.
141   Ibid.
142   Houts, 16.
143   Hewett, 187.
144   Ibid, 186.
145   Graham, 115.
146   Timmerman, 129.
147   Young, 710.
148   Sanderson, 116.
149   Crabtree, 133.
150   Marshall, 165.
151   John E. Brown, *The Fruit of the Spirit* (Siloam Springs: International Federation Publishing Co., 1918), 88.
152   Gage, 108.
153   Bethune, 136.
154   Crabtree, 134.
155   Winward, 167.
156   Sanderson, 116.
157   Hewett, 470.

158   Sanderson, 116.

159   William J. Bennett, *The Book of Virtues: A Treasury of Great Moral Stories* (New York: Simon & Schuster, 741.

160   Douglas, 368.

161   Houts, 11.

162   Elwell, 402.

163   Armitage, 47.

164   Barclay, 51–52.

165   Judith C. Lechman, *The Spirituality of Gentleness: Growing Toward Christian Wholeness* (San Francisco: Harper and Row, 1987), 2.

166   Reeve, 246.

167   Armitage, 48.

168   Lechman, 3.

169   Richards and Wakefield, 121.

170   Lechman, 13.

171   Sanderson, 133.

172   Brown, 102.

173   Houts, 16.

174   Brown, 59.

175   Gage, 85.

176   Richards and Wakefield, 120.

177   Hewett, 406.

178   M. Draper, 152.

179   Brown, 103.

180   Sanderson, 125.

181   Armitage, 72.

182   Ibid., 46.

183   Gage, 113.

184   Brown, 99.

185   Hewett, 229.

186   M. Draper, 428.

187   Ibid., 166.

188   Armitage, 73.

189   Bethune, 174

190   Gage, 119.

191   Hewett, 387.

192   Lechman, 20.

193   M. Draper, 151.

194 Hewett, 450.
195 Brown, 107.
196 Gage, 119–120.
197 Brown, 105.
198 Lechman, 11.
199 Timmerman, 149.
200 Douglas, 1085.
201 Graham, 281.
202 M. Draper, 50.
203 Winward, 199.
204 M. Draper, 166.
205 Ibid, 46.
206 Gage, 123.
207 Winward, 188.
208 Peter Thomas Geach, *The Virtues* (Cambridge: Cambridge University Press, 1977), 137.
209 M. Draper, 110.
210 Reeve, 293.
211 Armitage, 77.
212 Kesler, 51.
213 Olsson, 95.
214 Bethune, 178.
215 Armitage, 78.
216 Houts, 16.
217 Hewett, 476.
218 M. Draper, 54.
219 Ibid, 168.
220 Gage, 124.
221 Sanderson, 139.
     Richard P. Walters, *Counseling for Problems of Self-Control* (Dallas: Word Publishers, 1987), 195.
222 Walters, 194.
223 Timmerman, 147.
224 M. Draper, 167.
225 Bethune, 185.
226 Sanderson, 138.
227 M. Draper, 110.
228 Olsson, 96.

229 E. Draper, 11050.
230 Ibid, 11058.
231 Bethune, 185.
232 Reeve, 310–311.
233 Bethune, 208.
234 Gage, 124.
235 Barclay, 52.
236 M. Draper, 169.
237 Houts, 14.
238 Tan, 1256.
239 Phillips, 282.
240 Young, 382.